Come to *Me*

An Invitation from Jesus to Find Rest for Your Soul

MARY A. BOSWELL

Copyright © 2025 Mary A. Boswell

All rights reserved.

All Scripture quotations, unless otherwise noted, are taken from the ESV® Bible (The Holy Bible, English Standard Version®). ESV® Text Edition: 2016. Copyright © 2001 by Crossway, a publishing ministry of Good News Publishers. The ESV® text has been reproduced in cooperation with and by permission of Good News Publishers. Unauthorized reproduction of this publication is prohibited. All rights reserved.

Scripture quotations marked NIV are taken from the Holy Bible, New International Version®, NIV®. Copyright © 1973, 1978, 1984, 2011 by Biblica, Inc.™ Used by permission of Zondervan.

Scripture quotations taken from the Amplified® Bible (AMP), Copyright © 2015 by The Lockman Foundation. Used by permission. lockman.org.

The SBLGNT text itself is subject to the SBLGNT EULA and the morphological parsing and lemmatization is made available under a CC-BY-SA License.

Scripture quotations from The Authorized (King James) Version. Rights in the Authorized Version in the United Kingdom are vested in the Crown. Reproduced by permission of the Crown's Patentee, Cambridge University Press.

Scripture quotations taken from the (NASB®) New American Standard Bible®, Copyright © 1960, 1971, 1977, 1995, 2020 by The Lockman Foundation. Used by permission. All rights reserved. Lockman.org.

Scripture quoted by permission. All scripture quotations, unless otherwise indicated, are taken from the NET Bible® copyright © 1996-2006 by Biblical Studies Press, L.L.C. All rights reserved.

Scripture quotations marked (NLT) are taken from the *Holy Bible*, New Living Translation, copyright © 1996, 2004, 2007, Used by permission of Tyndale House Publishers Inc., Carol Stream, Illinois 60188. All rights reserved.

Edited by Jill Butler Wilson and Melanie Chitwood

Cover design and layout formatting by Nelly Murariu at PixBeeDesign.com.

Mom,

*Your heart to release your burdens to the Lord
and trust Him to walk with you to the ends of the earth and back,
left a legacy that will impact our family for generations to come.
Thank you for believing in my own legacy
and encouraging me to trust the Lord wherever He leads.*

CONTENTS

Introduction — vii
Focus Scripture — xi

WEEK 1: Come to Me — 1

Day 1: Finding God's Salvation Rest — 3
Day 2: Living in God's Daily Rest — 9
Day 3: Anticipating God's Ultimate Eternal Rest — 17
Day 4: Discovering Soul Rest Through a Divine Appointment — 23
Day 5: Review and Reflect — 28

WEEK 2: Take My Yoke Upon You — 31

Day 1: Choosing a Lighter Burden — 33
Day 2: Remembering We Are Known and Held by God — 40
Day 3: Building the Strength to Cast Our Burdens — 46
Day 4: Approaching the Throne of Grace with Honesty — 51
Day 5: Review and Reflect — 57

WEEK 3: Learn from Me — 59

Day 1: Learning from Jesus's Examples — 61
Day 2: Finding Comfort and Rest in the Gentleness of God — 68
Day 3: Drawing Courage from God's Sovereignty — 73
Day 4: Feeling God's Nearness in Our Time of Need — 79
Day 5: Review and Reflect — 85

WEEK 4: Find Rest for Your Soul   **87**

Day 1: Trusting the Holy Spirit and Jesus to Intercede for Us   89

Day 2: Fixing Our Eyes on the Eternal Glory of God   94

Day 3: Regaining Our Strength   100

Day 4: Remaining Clear-Headed and Watchful as We Move Forward in Hope   106

Day 5: Review and Reflect   112

Study Review and Reflection   115
A Final Word   117
Acknowledgments   119
Leader Guide   121
Author Bio   129

Introduction

While I couldn't understand her words, the lines on her forehead, dark circles under her eyes, and slumped shoulders spoke volumes. My heart felt the weariness and exhaustion that emanated from her body. The translator explained to our mission group that Marcella was worried about her daughter, Dina, who was extremely sick from dengue fever. Marcella, a single mom with three kids, worked hard to provide her family with the necessities of life. Now, she struggled to balance working while caring for her daughter.

Despite her exhaustion, Marcella trusted that the Lord would give her the strength and endurance she needed. She asked us to pray for her and Dina.

Oh, how my heart broke for Marcella as I stood next to Dina's bed praying while my healthy daughter, who was just a year older than Dina, stood beside me. Despite the language barrier, our hearts were knit together as two moms who love our families, diligently work to care for them and serve the Lord wherever He leads.

Marcella was not the only woman in Guatemala who struggled with the weight of her burdens to the point of weariness and exhaustion. Women throughout the village fed and raised their children, worked in the fields, and maintained the home while their husbands worked either as day laborers or for months in another country. Just as each woman balanced a heavy jar of water or a basket of clothes on her head and carried her wrapped baby or toddler securely on her back, she also bore a heavy load of worry, exhaustion, and stress upon her shoulders.

While you and I may not live in a remote village in Guatemala, we, too, know what it feels like to carry the weight of worry and overwhelm as we attempt to juggle our lives' concerns. There are days when caring for a sick loved one or chasing after active toddlers drain our last bit of energy. And there are moments when fear threatens to overtake us in the uncertainty of financial hardship or job change.

Friend, who is overwhelmed by the weight of worry, I want you to know that I see you. I know where you are because I've been there too. I've struggled with being so overwhelmed from trying to hold it all together in my day-to-day life that I forgot how to release my burdens to the Lord. I thought that if I took a deep breath and put on my big girl pants, I could handle the grief of caring for my mom with terminal cancer, performing all the household duties while my husband was working full time and in school full time for a Doctoral degree, and parenting two teenagers all through the COVID-19 pandemic.

Without realizing it, I built a wall around my heart. That wall was a protective barrier to keep me from feeling grief, heartache, and exhaustion. I thought I trusted the Lord with everything but mainly lived on adrenaline and willpower for years. Upon my mom's death, my husband's graduation and decreased stress for him at work, and my children finding their way through the COVID-19 pandemic aftermath, the overwhelming stress decreased.

At this point, I realized just how broken I was because of my self-reliance.

Instead of relying on the Lord to carry me through those difficult years, I'd kept my worries to myself, and over time, the weight of the burdens had threatened to crush me.

But, thankfully, in His infinite love and compassion, the Lord led me to Matthew 11:28-30 during an early morning quiet time, "'Come to me, all you who labor and are heavy laden, and I will give you rest. Take my yoke upon you, and learn from me, for I am gentle and lowly in heart, and you will find rest for your souls. For my yoke is easy, and my burden is light'"(ESV).

Through Jesus's words, I realized the Lord had never left me. He had been with me all along and was still with me, ready to take my burdens upon Himself and help me find rest for my soul. I just needed to learn how to release those worries to Him. Through studying God's Word, praying, and journaling, I learned how to experience the peace and rest that comes from Him.

Sister in struggle, just like He did for me, the Lord wants to take the exhaustion you feel from your burdens upon Himself and help you find rest for your soul. As you walk through this study, you will learn how to accept His invitation to come to Him and release your burdens through daily time in His Word, listening to the Holy Spirit during prayer, and releasing the stress of life through journaling.

During each of the four weeks of study, you will study small portions of our focal verse along with other supporting scripture. Each day will begin with **A Note from Life** that will help you know you are not alone in the difficulties you face each day. You will spend time in **Scripture Study** exploring and unpacking the truths from God's Word as you gain greater insight into His character. And each day will close out with an **Application** section, encouraging you to personally engage with and apply lessons you have learned in your daily study. Each week will end with a **Review and Reflect** day that will help you bring all that you have learned for the week together.

As you begin to experience relief, renewed joy, and strength, I want you to know that there will always be things in your life that cause you worry and stress. But, as you begin to release your burdens and allow God to carry them, you will find strength in Him and develop the perseverance to continue trusting the Lord.

Focus Scripture

I'm so glad you are undertaking this journey toward rest. This study is designed to provide you a framework for digging into different portions of Matthew 11:28-30 over the next four weeks. For this study, I've chosen to focus on the English Standard Version of that Bible passage:

"Come to me, all you who labor and are heavy laden, and I will give you rest. Take my yoke upon you, and learn from me, for I am gentle and lowly in heart, and you will find rest for your souls. For my yoke is easy, and my burden is light."

Because considering the original text and reading and studying multiple translations of a passage helps us better understand what God tells us through His written Word, I include several different translations here. There are multiple instances throughout the study where we unpack the original Greek language so you'll notice the first translation I share is the original Greek of this passage. As you read through the translations, notice the various nuances that stand out to you.

> "δεῦτε πρός με πάντες οἱ κοπιῶντες καὶ πεφορτισμένοι κἀγὼ ἀναπαύσω ὑμᾶς. ἄρατε τὸν ζυγόν μου ἐφ' ὑμᾶς καὶ μάθετε ἀπ' ἐμοῦ ὅτι πραΰς εἰμι καὶ ταπεινὸς τῇ καρδίᾳ καὶ εὑρήσετε ἀνάπαυσιν ταῖς ψυχαῖς ὑμῶν. ὁ γὰρ ζυγός μου χρηστὸς καὶ τὸ φορτίον μου ἐλαφρόν ἐστιν."
>
> (Matthew 11:30 MGNT)

> "Come unto me, all ye that labour and are heavy laden, and I will give you rest. Take my yoke upon you, and learn of me; for I am meek and lowly in heart: and ye shall find rest unto your souls. For my yoke is easy, and my burden is light." (KJV)

"Come to Me, all who are weary and burdened and I will give you rest. Take My yoke upon you and learn from ME, for I am gentle and humble in heart, and YOU WILL FIND REST FOR YOUR SOULS. For My yoke is comfortable, and MY burden is light." (NASB20)

"Come to me, all you who are weary and burdened, and I will give you rest. Take my yoke on you and learn from me, because I am gentle and humble in heart, and you will find rest for your souls. For my yoke is easy to bear, and my load is not hard to carry." (NET)

"Come to me, all you who are weary and burdened, and I will give you rest. Take my yoke upon you and learn from me, for I am gentle and humble in heart, and you will find rest for your souls. For my yoke is easy and my burden is light." (NIV)

"Then Jesus said, 'Come to me, all of you who are weary and carry heavy burdens, and I will give you rest. Take my yoke upon you. Let me teach you, because I am humble and gentle at heart, and you will find rest for your souls. For my yoke is easy to bear, and the burden I give you is light.'" (NLT)

Before you begin your first week of study, write Matthew 11:28-30 in your favorite translation. Underline any words or phrases that stand out to you.

_____

_____

_____

_____

_____

Circle the words below that reflect what you think true rest for the soul might look like for you. Add any other words and phrases that reflect your vision of rest in the space provided.

Physical Rest

Recreation

Tranquility of Soul

Peace

Calm

Love

Healing

On the scale below, circle the number that indicates how possible true rest seems right now?

1   2   3   4   5   6   7   8   9   10

Complete the sentence: I could find true rest if…

WEEK 1

Come to Me

Welcome to week one of *Come to Me: An Invitation from Jesus to Find Rest for Your Soul*. This week's focus is on Matthew 11:28, "'Come to me, all who labor and are heavy laden, and I will give you rest.'" When studying God's Word, it's always best to start with understanding the passage's context.

Jesus opened His invitation in Matthew 11:28 with the three words, "'Come to me....'" The Greek word for "come" is *duete*, an imperative that means "Come here!" or "Come now!" Jesus also uses the same word in Matthew 4:19 when He calls His first disciples to "'Follow me . . . .'"[i] John 1:35-42 tells us that Andrew and Simon Peter had previously encountered Jesus when they were with John the Baptist. While the disciples weren't fully aware of the adventures and strife they would face, they understood that Jesus was the Messiah Moses wrote about in the Old Testament, and upon Jesus's invitation, they immediately left their nets and followed Him.

In Matthew 11, Jesus talked to the crowd, whose questions and doubts were growing. He explained that God, the Father, revealed Himself to Jesus, and Jesus would reveal Himself to whom He chose. However, those who, in their arrogance, thought themselves too wise and didn't need God wouldn't understand. But those who were like children and recognized their weakness and need for dependence on God would hear Jesus's call and come to Him for rest.

Not only did Jesus invite the disciples and crowd to come and follow Him, but today, through God's Word, He's also inviting us to do the same. But who are we? Are we the ones who think we're too wise to need God, or are we like the children who recognize our weakness and need for dependence on God?

When we answer Jesus's call, we answer God's invitation to rest in Him. He desires to give us rest and learn from Him how to live no longer weary and burdened in three ways. This week's study will unpack three different kinds of rest that we receive upon accepting His invitation:

1. We find **Salvation Rest** in the saving knowledge and acceptance of Jesus as our Lord and Savior.

2. We enjoy **Daily Rest** when we lay our burdens before Him and learn from Him as He carries our burdens.

3. We experience **Eternal Rest** when God calls us to be with Him in Heaven at the end of our lives.[ii]

How does knowing that Jesus calls you to come to Him make you feel?

DAY 1

Finding God's Salvation Rest

📖 A NOTE FROM LIFE

I love God's perfect timing because today, as I write this note to you, it's also Passover Thursday. Today, so many years ago, Jesus sat among His disciples to share His last meal with them. Jesus knew that not only was He surrounded by friends, but among them sat an enemy who would soon betray Him and lead to His arrest, torture, and death. Jesus obediently carried the weight and burden of what would come because He knew that soon He would also take the weight and burden of the world's sins upon Himself.

But, despite that knowledge, He broke bread and shared wine with those at the table, giving thanks for the body that would be broken and the blood that would be spilled in atonement for not only the sins of the world, but also for you and me.

Friend, Jesus willingly took on the sin that threatens to crush us. He took on the weight of the heartache, pain, fear, and grief that burdens us because He desired to give us the true salvation rest that God wanted for each of us. And because God loved us so much, He knew that could only come through the death of His perfect Son, Jesus.

📖 SCRIPTURE STUDY

Today, as you begin your study, you will explore how God gives you salvation rest as you walk with Him through a saving faith in Christ.

God's Word tells us in John 3:16, "For God so loved the world that he gave his one and only Son, that whoever believes in him shall not perish but have eternal life." God loved each one of us so much that He sent His one and only Son to earth to bear the burden of our sins. He took that sin upon Himself and experienced cruel punishment and death on the cross. Then, three days later, He rose from the grave.

✝ What does it mean to know that God loved YOU so much that He gave His only Son to die on the cross for your sins?

_____

_____

_____

_____

✝ Look up John 14:6. Who does Jesus say He is?

_____

_____

_____

_____

✝ Read Acts 4:11-13. Where does Peter tell us salvation comes from?

_____

_____

_____

_____

Day 1: Finding God's Salvation Rest

✝ Read 2 Corinthians 6:2. When does Paul tell us is the time for salvation?

_____

_____

_____

✝ Read the two translations of Matthew 11:28 below and underline the words or phrases that indicate who Jesus calls to Him.

> "Come to me, all who labor and are heavy laden, and I will give you rest." (Matthew 11:28 ESV)

> "Come to me, all who are weary and burdened, and I will give you rest." (Matthew 11:28 NIV)

✝ Why does Jesus call us to come to Him?

_____

_____

_____

_____

Before moving forward, it's important to understand the terms "labor" and "heavy laden." The Greek word for "labor" is *kapiao*, which means "to grow weary, tired, and exhausted, carrying heavy burdens or grief." [iii] The Greek word for "heavy laden" is *phortizo*, which means "to place or load a burden upon something or someone."[iv]

Jesus was talking to Jews who lived under the burdensome weight of the Mosaic law and tradition of the Old Covenant. They worked hard to please God, but Jesus was calling them to Himself because He was the

New Covenant. Jesus wanted them to understand they didn't have to work hard to overcome their sin. Instead, they could release the heavy burden of their sin to Him and receive salvation rest.

To understand this better, let's look briefly at the Old Covenant versus the New Covenant. In Deuteronomy 9:11, Moses wrote, "And at the end of forty days and forty nights the Lord gave me the two tablets of stone, the tablets of the covenant." These stone tablets, known as the Ten Commandments, instructed the people how to live. But the people couldn't live perfectly under the law. Because of this, the Lord established His New Covenant through Jesus Christ. The Apostle John tells us in John 1:17, "For the law was given through Moses; grace and truth came through Jesus Christ." In Luke 22:20, Luke explains, "In the same way, after the supper he took the cup, saying, 'This cup is the new covenant in my blood, which is poured out for you.'"

Society tells us that we must strive and work hard to be good, but because of Jesus, we no longer have to strive to be "good enough" according to God's law or any other. We are sinners in need of a Savior who willingly took our burdens upon Himself to give us the gift of salvation rest.

🙏 APPLICATION

The Apostle Paul wrote in Romans 10:9, "because, if you confess with your mouth that Jesus is Lord and believe in your heart that God raised him from the dead, you will be saved." When we admit that we don't have it all together and are sinners and ask for His forgiveness, He forgives our sins. That's when we begin our walk with the Lord.

Confessing sin, asking for forgiveness, and accepting Jesus as our Lord and Savior is the foundation of finding rest in Christ. This is a one-time act. But because we live in a fallen world, we experience pressures, cares, and concerns that can muddy or cloud our clear vision of salvation rest, causing us to drift away from the peace we experience as we allow Jesus to carry our burdens. When that happens, Jesus calls us to come back to Him and release those burdens back to Him.

And friend, my heart and desire is that you will do just that as you journey through this study.

✝ As you close your first day of study, take time in the space below to share the concerns that weigh heavily on your heart with the Lord.

_____

_____

_____

_____

_____

_____

✝ If you've already accepted Jesus as your personal Lord and Savior and have been saved write a prayer of thanksgiving to the Lord.

_____

_____

_____

_____

_____

_____

If you have not been saved I invite you to close your time with this prayer.

Heavenly Father, thank You for loving me so much that You sent Your Son to die on the cross for my sins. Lord, I confess that I'm a sinner needing Your saving grace. Forgive me for turning to other things for comfort and strength. When the pressures of this world cloud my vision of Your salvation rest, remind me of Your love and desire to carry the burdens that weigh me down. Give me a heart that seeks You and the peace that comes from You. In Jesus's name, amen.

I'll see you back here tomorrow as we continue finding rest in the Lord.

DAY 2

Living in God's Daily Rest

📖 A NOTE FROM LIFE

Yesterday, you worked through the salvation rest that comes from confessing your sins and trusting Jesus as your Lord and Savior. That was the first step. Today's study explores living in the daily rest that comes from accepting the Lord's invitation to come to Him and learn from Him as He carries your burdens. Through the Lord's personal invitation to come to Him, He desires to show you how to rest and live a life of joy in Him.

Living a life of rest and joy starts with taking an inventory of your tasks and releasing those that are not yours to carry. For example, have you said yes to a request from a friend or an activity at your child's school that you can turn over to someone else? Or has your family calendar become so overloaded with multiple activities that you're all running on fumes?

I realize saying no to people and opportunities can be very hard. Before you continue with today's study consider these questions.

✝ Why do you think you say yes to almost everything?

_____

_____

_____

_____

✝ What/Who is hard for you to say no to?

_____

_____

_____

_____

_____

✝ What do you think would happen if you said no to a request that you don't feel called to do?

_____

_____

_____

_____

_____

On the other hand, there are responsibilities that you don't have the luxury of surrendering entirely because you are the only person who can carry those concerns, such as providing for and raising your children, caring for a sick loved one, or fulfilling duties in your career. When those responsibilities and worries begin to weigh you down, it's time to ask Jesus to take the heavy load off your shoulders and carry them with you.

SCRIPTURE STUDY

Three passages in the Bible give us examples of laying down burdens and concerns and placing complete trust in God.

✝ Read Psalm 31:1-8 and fill in the chart below. I've given you an example for each column.

What does David ask the Lord to do?	What does the Lord do? Who is the Lord to David?	What does David do?
vs. 1 – "...let me never be put to shame..."	vs. 3 – "...you are my rock and my fortress..."	vs. 5 – "Into your hand I commit my spirit..."

King David wrote Psalm 31 during a time of deep distress and opened by proclaiming his trust in the refuge of the Lord, who would never let him down. He called on the Lord to hear him and be his rock of refuge and strong fortress in his time of need. As David committed his spirit to the Lord, He saw David's distress and faithfully led David to safety.

✝ Read Luke 23:44-46 below and circle words or phrases that stand out. Then, read the passage a second time and highlight Jesus's words.

> "It was now about the sixth hour, and there was darkness over the whole land until the ninth hour, while the sun's light failed. And the curtain of the temple was torn in two. Then Jesus, calling out with a loud voice, said, 'Father, into your hands I commit my spirit!' And having said this he breathed his last."
>
> (Luke 23:44-46 ESV)

Darkness covered the earth, signifying the battle between God and Satan during the crucifixion. In Matthew 27:51b, we read, "The earth shook, and the rocks split," as the temple curtain tore in two from top to bottom. The curtain prevented the people from entering the Most Holy Place and the Presence of God. Just before Jesus took His last breath, He quoted David's words from Psalm 31:5, "Father, into your hands I commit my spirit!"

While all seemed lost, Jesus rose from the grave three days later. His death paid the penalty for our sins, and His resurrection gave us direct access to God.

✝ Read Acts 7:59-60 below. Circle who Stephen cried out to, and underline what he called out.

> "And as they were stoning Stephen, he called out, 'Lord Jesus, receive my spirit.' And falling to his knees he cried out with a loud voice, 'Lord, do not hold this sin against them.' And when he had said this, he fell asleep."

Stephen was under extreme persecution by the religious leaders known as the Sanhedrin, who were enraged by what Stephen had just told them. But despite his dire circumstances, he still looked to Jesus, who was "... standing at the right hand of God..." (Acts 7:55). While being stoned, Stephen cried out and asked Jesus to receive his spirit, and he died.

✝ What commonality do you see in Luke 23:44-46, Psalm 31:5, and Acts 7:59-60?

___

___

___

___

In all three passages, we see three men who experienced grief, ridicule, pain, and sorrow. Yet, in the weight of their deep distress, they cried out and committed their spirit to God, who faithfully heard their plea and was with them.

David experienced God's steadfast love (Psalm 31:21). Jesus entered God's presence as He took His final breath (Luke 23:46) and had the joy of doing His Father's will (John 6:38-40). And Stephen was blessed as he "... gazed into Heaven and saw the glory of God, and Jesus standing at the right hand of God" (Acts 7:55).

APPLICATION

Today, we've learned how three men experienced true rest as they released their deep distress to the Lord. Friend, what weighs you down? Are you heartbroken over a loved one's choices? Does the stress of feeding your family or the worry of a family member's health threaten to overwhelm you?

The Lord wants you to lay that at His feet through prayer. He wants to relieve you of that burden so He can take it upon His shoulders and carry the heavy load as you walk through life with Him. And as He carries that load, you will experience rest and joy in Him.

Today, I want to give you permission to rest. Sit with the Lord and release what weighs heavily on your heart. Let Him come alongside you and carry the heavy load as He gives you His peace and comfort.

† As you close out today, take some time in the space below to write down the burdens that weigh heavily on your heart.

_____

_____

_____

_____

_____

_____

_____

_____

✝ Make a list of obligations and activites that fill your schedule.

✝ Review the list above, note any obligations that aren't yours to carry, and commit to handing those over to someone else this week.

Heavenly Father, I'm tired and worn out from all the striving and worry. In Your Word, You tell me to come to You and get away with You. Please show me how to rest in You and remind me each day to release my worries and concerns to You. Reveal the areas of my life where I need to say no, so I can make space to focus on the things and people You have given me as my responsibility. And help me to release the weight of my burdens so that You can come alongside me and help carry the heavy load. Thank You for the gift of Your presence, which has brought me peace, comfort, and joy. In Jesus's name, amen.

DAY 3

Anticipating God's Ultimate Eternal Rest

📖 A NOTE FROM LIFE

My husband and I lead a thriving group of adults through the study of Scripture every Sunday morning. One morning during his teaching, Jeff made a statement that caught my breath. He stated, "For the believer, this world will be the worst they ever have to endure. For the non-believer, it is the best they can ever hope for."

I don't know about you, but it brings me so much peace to realize that the heaviness I feel under the weight of life's difficulties won't last forever. Yes, grief over the loss of a loved one is sometimes more than I think I can bear, and the worry that fills my chest over the actions of a child threatens to steal my breath. BUT GOD! He knew the fallen world we live in would be hard for us, and He planned to redeem the pain and give us a beautiful, eternal rest with Him in heaven.

📖 SCRIPTURE STUDY

Yesterday's study unpacked what it means to have daily rest and how to experience it in Jesus. Today, you will start at the very beginning as you explore what it means to have Eternal Rest in heaven.

✝ Read Genesis 1:26-2:3 in your Bible.

† Who did God create on the sixth day? And why did He create them?

_____

_____

_____

_____

† What did God do on the seventh day?

_____

_____

_____

God didn't need to rest because He was tired. Instead, His creation was complete, and His desire was for all creation to rest with Him in paradise. But Adam and Eve's disobedience and sin of eating the fruit from the tree of knowledge of good and evil (Genesis 3:1-13) brought the fall of humanity and resulted in banishment from the Garden of Eden (Genesis 3:21-22). Their disobedience led to a life of toil and hardship for all of humanity.

Adam and Eve missed the gift of rest with their Heavenly Father in the Garden of Eden. But God still wanted His children to experience His perfect rest.

Day 3: Anticipating God's Ultimate Eternal Rest

✝ Read Hebrews 4:1-11 in your Bible. What was the promise of rest?

_____

_____

_____

_____

The author of Hebrews referenced the rest God promised the Israelites upon entering the land of Canaan after traveling through the wilderness (Numbers 14:5-9). God used Moses to rescue His people from the bondage of slavery and deliver them to the promised rest of the land of Canaan. However, only Joshua and Caleb believed that God would do what He had promised and deliver the land to them. Because of their unbelief, the rest of the Israelites spent years wandering on the edge of the Promised Land and would never enter the promised rest of God. In contrast, God allowed Joshua and Caleb to lead the next generation into the Promised Land.

✝ Write out Hebrews 4:8-9 in the space below.

_____

_____

_____

_____

_____

Neither Moses nor Joshua could give the rest God desired for the Israelites, us, and ultimately all of humanity.

✝ Read Hebrews 3:3-6 below. Underline God's faithful servant and circle the One counted worthy and found faithful over God's house.

"For Jesus has been counted worthy of more glory than Moses – as much more glory as the builder of a house has more honor than the house itself. (For every house is built by someone, but the builder of all things is God.) Now Moses was faithful in all God's house as a servant, to testify to the things that were to be spoken later, but Christ is faithful over God's house as a son. And we are his house, if indeed we hold fast our confidence and our boasting in our hope." (Hebrews 3:3-6)

✝ Why does the author of Hebrews declare that we are God's house?

_____

_____

_____

Humanity would endure much heartache, but God had a plan to redeem us. In Genesis 3:15, God told the serpent, "I will put enmity between you and the woman, and between your offspring and her offspring...."

✝ Who did God put enmity (hostility, animosity, and hatred) between?

_____

_____

_____

_____

The King James Version refers to offspring as seed. *The Bible Knowledge Commentary* explains, "the 'offspring' of the woman was Cain, then all humanity at large, and then Christ and those collectively in Him. The 'offspring' of the serpent includes demons and anyone serving his kingdom of darkness, those whose 'father' is the devil."[v] It's interesting to note that throughout the Bible, we most often see references to offspring or seed through the male lineage. But here, the reference is to Eve, who creates the lineage, starting with Cain, moving throughout humanity, and continuing to the virgin birth of Jesus Christ. This passage is the first to mention the Gospel of Jesus, known as the Protoevangelium.

✝ Read Genesis 3:15b in the ESV and NIV versions and underline what will happen.

> Genesis 3:15b, ". . . he shall bruise your head, and you shall bruise his heel."(ESV)

> Genesis 3:15b, ". . . he will crush your head, and you will strike his heel." (NIV)

God sent Jesus to rescue us from the bondage of sin and deliver us to salvation rest in God so that we can experience daily rest from Him and ultimate eternal rest with Him. While Satan bruised Jesus with His death on the cross, three days later, Jesus crushed Satan with His resurrection, providing our salvation rest. However, ultimately, Jesus will crush Satan once and for all (Revelation 19:19-20; Revelation 20:10) when He returns in ultimate victory as God creates an eternal paradise and rest for His children (Revelation 21:1-4; Revelation 22:1-3).

APPLICATION

Today, we explored humanity's fall and God's plan to redeem us. While we can only imagine what heaven will be like, the expectation of eternal rest can give us peace when we are overwhelmed with life's struggles and ease fears of death for ourselves and our loved ones who have accepted salvation rest.

✝ In the space below, take a few minutes to write down what you imagine heaven will be like in contrast to the struggles you face today.

___

___

___

___

___

___

Heavenly Father, thank You for desiring for all of creation to rest with You in paradise. And thank You that when sin entered the world, You had a plan from the very beginning to redeem us so that we can have eternal rest with You. When I am overwhelmed by the harshness of the world, remind me that you have a perfect plan, and as Your child, I will one day live in the reality of Your perfect glory. In Jesus's name, amen.

DAY 4

Discovering Soul Rest through a Divine Appointment

📖 A NOTE FROM LIFE

During the mission trip to Guatemala that I mentioned in the study's introduction, our team had an opportunity to build a house for a single mom and her five children. The laughter and joy we experienced as we tried to communicate in our broken Spanish and their broken English knit our hearts together.

The translator explained that Teresa felt seen by someone for the first time in more years than she could count. My eyes rested on the well she used to draw water for her family, and my heart broke for her and the struggles she faced each day. The well was a small opening surrounded by several layers of stones just tall enough to prevent a small child from falling over the edge. A makeshift rope and pulley were attached to a bucket that brought muddy water from the hole. Once the bucket was raised from the well, the muddy water was transferred into a jar that Teresa used to fill the concrete container where she washed her family's clothes.

As I surveyed the scene before me, I couldn't help but think about another woman sitting at a well who had a divine appointment with Jesus.

SCRIPTURE STUDY

✝ Read John 4:1-15 in your Bible and write down words or phrases that stand out to you in the space provided.

_____

_____

_____

_____

In our reading today, we see a woman who is sweaty and weary from a dusty walk in the sweltering heat of the noonday sun. She quietly began drawing water from the well. She hoped the man at the well would ignore her, but her hopes were dashed as He asked her for a drink of water. "You are a Jew and I am a Samaritan woman. How can you ask me for a drink?" she questioned. Jesus answered her, "If you knew the gift of God and who it is that asks you for a drink, you would have asked him and he would have given you living water" (John 4:9-10 NIV).

It's important to gain some context before we dig deeper into this passage. Jews despised Samaritans and viewed them as half-breeds who emerged after the Assyrians conquered the northern kingdom of Israel and the Babylonians conquered the southern kingdom of Judah. In both cases, only the lowest classes of Jewish society were left behind when the Jews were taken into exile. Those left behind intermarried with non-Jews and, over time, formed their own ethnic and religious group. The Jews' dislike for the Samaritans was so great that they would take a longer route around Samaria to travel from Jerusalem to Galilee.

John 4:4 tells us that Jesus "... had to pass through Samaria." He could've traveled around Samaria like everyone else, but Jesus knew people in Samaria needed Him. More specifically, He had a divine appointment with the woman at the well.

Day 4: Discovering Soul Rest Through a Divine Appointment

Most women drew their water from the well in the cool morning hours, but this woman came alone at the hottest part of the day. Not only was she a Samaritan, but she was also an outcast because of her life choices. But Jesus reached out first and asked for a drink.

✝ Have there been times when you have felt like an outcast? If you were the Samaritan woman at the well with Jesus, how would you feel if He acknowledged you and asked for a drink?

_____

_____

_____

_____

While the woman knew she shouldn't talk to Him, her heart cried out to understand more of what this man was saying. Her curiosity was piqued, and she let down her guard and began talking with Jesus, seeking to understand what He was saying.

✝ What question did she ask Jesus in John 4:11-12?

_____

_____

_____

_____

Patiently, Jesus listened to her questions and lovingly addressed her deepest needs. "Jesus answered, 'Everyone who drinks this water will be thirsty again, but whoever drinks the water I give him will never thirst. Indeed, the water I give him will become in him a spring of water welling up to eternal life'" (John 4:13).

The Samaritan woman came to the well thirsty and needed physical nourishment, but Jesus was there to fulfill a more profound need—to serve her spiritual thirst and hunger.

Women have many responsibilities that leave us both physically and spiritually dry. Each day, we tend to our family's needs and diligently work where God leads us to work and serve. We care for those in need and desire to help others find relief from their burdens. But as we help others, we carry the weight of our burdens upon us until we are weary and exhausted both physically and spiritually. As much as we may try, we can't care for those around us if we are physically and spiritually dry.

In Isaiah 55:1-2, 6, we read God's invitation to those who are thirsty.

✝ Underline any words or phrases that stand out in the passages below.

> "Come, all you who are thirsty, come to the waters; and you who have no money, come, buy and eat! Come, buy wine and milk without money and without cost. Why spend money on what is not bread, and your labor on what does not satisfy? Listen, listen to me, and eat what is good, and your soul will delight in the richest of fair." (Isaiah 55:1-2)

> "Seek the Lord while he may be found; call on him while he is near." (Isaiah 55:6)

Instead of drawing muddy water from the well of this world, God invites us to come to Him through Jesus, who provides true life-sustaining nourishment to quench our spiritual thirst.

APPLICATION

When you accept the invitation to sit with Jesus, read His Word, and listen with your mind and soul, you actively participate in your divine appointment with God.

✝ What or who do you turn to for comfort rather than turning to the Lord?

_____

_____

_____

_____

_____

✝ Imagine you're the woman sitting at the well with Jesus. In the space provided, share with Him what you need physically, emotionally, and spiritually.

_____

_____

_____

_____

Heavenly Father, thank You for seeing me and the thirst within my soul for nourishment and rest. As I sit with You and lay my burdens before You, please give me Your life-sustaining peace and relief. Help me feel Your presence as You walk this journey with me. In Jesus's name, amen.

DAY 5

Review and Reflect

Heavenly Father, thank You for the invitation to come to You so that You can give me rest. As I spent time in Your Word this week, I realized my deep need for complete rest in You spiritually as I rest in Your saving grace, daily as I release the burdens that weigh heavily upon my heart, and in the future as I await eternal rest with You in heaven. Give me a heart that seeks the divine appointment You have for me each day so that You can fulfill my spiritual thirst and hunger. In Jesus's name, amen.

Thank you for joining me on this journey as you learn to accept the Lord's invitation to come and release your burdens to Him so that you can experience peace and rest while you labor through life with Him.

✝ During day one, you recognized the Lord's invitation to come to Him for rest as you explored His call for Salvation Rest.

✝ On day two, you unpacked Daily Rest by studying three passages that gave examples of laying down burdens and concerns and placing complete trust in God.

✝ On day three, you studied God's plan for redemption and Eternal Rest by returning to the beginning, humanity's fall in the Garden of Eden.

✝ During day four, you studied the story of a woman who had a divine appointment with Jesus and learned that He was there to fill more than just a physical need. He was there to fill her spiritual thirst and hunger. Like the woman at the well, He also has a divine appointment with you to fill your spiritual thirst and hunger.

APPLICATION

† Take a few minutes to review how the Lord spoke to you each day. Write out the passage that spoke to your heart this week.

_____

_____

_____

_____

_____

† Journal a prayer to the Lord based on the passage above.

_____

_____

_____

_____

_____

† Review your daily application questions and journal how the Lord ministered to your spiritual and physical needs this week.

_____

_____

_____

_____

_____

WEEK 2

Take My Yoke Upon You

Welcome back to week two of *Come to Me: An Invitation from Jesus to Find Rest for Your Soul*. This week's focus is on the short phrase, "Take my yoke upon you" from Matthew 11:29.

Jesus tells us to take His yoke upon ourselves. The Greek word for "take" is *Airo*, which means "to place on oneself," and the Greek word for "yoke" is *zygos*, meaning "to join, bind, in order to pull together."

A physical yoke is a heavy wooden harness that fits over the shoulders of oxen and is attached to the equipment carried by the oxen. One ox can bear its body weight, between 1,500 and 3,000 pounds, but when a yoke connects two oxen, they can bear a combined weight of approximately 13,000 pounds. By working together, the load is more manageable.

In the same way that two oxen connected with a physical yoke can carry a larger load, the heavy load you carry is much more manageable when you allow Jesus to come alongside you as you take His yoke upon your shoulders.

But to pick something up, we must first lay down what we already carry and then set aside our will as we live surrendered to His Lordship and learn from Him as we live according to His will. Through your study this week, God's Word will help you fully understand the Lord's desire to carry your burdens and learn how to release those burdens as you take up His yoke.

DAY 1

Choosing a Lighter Burden

📖 A NOTE FROM LIFE

Before our kids were born, I was a critical care nurse who loved the action and mental challenge of caring for very ill patients. I also thrived on the connection and ministry opportunities I had with families and loved ones in their greatest time of need.

As much as I loved my nursing career, I knew God called me to stay home and raise our children. So, when we started our family, I hung up my stethoscope and became a stay-at-home mom. The transition was much harder than I expected. Don't get me wrong; I was grateful for the opportunity to be with my children and provide for their daily needs. But as a young stay-at-home mom, I remember the pressure I put on myself to do "all the things" and the need to be successful in the eyes of the world.

I listened to the voices that pushed me to have our young toddlers in play groups, Kindermusik, and story time at the library so they would grow into well-rounded kids. As soon as they were old enough, I signed them up for the local sports leagues, dance, and gymnastics. And as a Christian, I also knew the importance of raising our kids on God's Word and being part of a local church, which meant we were at church every time the doors opened.

As my children grew older, I equated my success as a mom with their accomplishments at school and in extracurricular activities. And without realizing it, I fell into the trap of believing I was a "good Christian mom" because our family was one of the volunteer families our church could always count on to help. After years of working hard to live up to self-imposed expectations, I was exhausted and struggled to withstand the weight of the schedules and responsibilities.

Friend, I wonder if, like me, you are exhausted from years of striving to live up to the lies of the world that say you and your family must do it all for you to be a successful mom. Today, you will dig into God's Word and learn how He wants you to live a life free from striving and rest in who He has truly called you to be.

 SCRIPTURE STUDY

Studying Matthew 23:1-12 helps us understand how Jesus's yoke lightens our heavy load.

✝ Let's start by reading Matthew 23:1-7 in your Bible and fill out the chart below.

What do the Pharisees do and say?	What don't the Pharisees do?	Why do the Pharisees do their deeds?

Day 1: Choosing a Lighter Burden

As Jesus addressed the crowd and His disciples, He contrasted God-honoring behavior with how the Scribes and Pharisees behaved. The Scribes and Pharisees quickly told people how to live but didn't practice what they preached. Instead, they created heavy burdens for the people as they added to the Ten Commandments (Exodus 20:1-17) and the law of Moses, creating extra laws that were impossible for the people to live up to. Jesus also noted that the Scribes and Pharisees wanted to bring attention to themselves by adorning their robes with ornate phylacteries, which were leather boxes containing scrolls with scripture and were attached to the head and arm with leather straps. Prayer tassels were attached to the fringes of their robes. They also desired to sit in the most honored positions at feasts and synagogues, such as Moses' seat, which was a raised chair where the Rabbi sat to deliver a sermon in the synagogue.

✝ Read Matthew 23:8-12. How does Jesus remind His followers that greatness is determined?

_____

_____

_____

_____

✝ Read 1 John 5:1-5. First John 5:2 says, when we love God, we will obey His commandments. In verse three, it says that His commandments aren't burdensome. Do you believe that God's commandments aren't burdensome? Write your thoughts below.

_____

_____

_____

_____

✝ Read Deuteronomy 6:4-9. How are we to love God?

_____
_____
_____
_____
_____

✝ How are we to keep the commandments on our hearts daily?

_____
_____
_____
_____
_____

I recognize that living up to the commandments of God can seem overwhelming and burdensome. Especially when we live in a world that says we must be perfect in everything we do. But remember, God gave us Jesus, the New Covenant, to take the weight of our burdens. Matthew 22:37-39 summarizes Deuteronomy 4:5 and Leviticus 19:18 by encouraging us to love God with all our heart, soul, and mind as we love our neighbor.

When we live a life of humility that seeks to honor God and others, we're less likely to fall under the weight of burdens imposed by ourselves and the world. God didn't give commandments to weigh us down but to show us how to live a life free from striving to be the perfect person and have a perfect, carefree life.

† Write 1 John 5:4-5 in the space below.

_____

_____

_____

_____

† How can we gain victory over the burdens that weigh us down?

_____

_____

_____

_____

These two verses give us the encouragement we need. Jesus defeated Satan through His death on the cross. We can experience victory and joy because Jesus has overcome the enemy. And through our faith in Christ, we overcome the pressures to be the perfect mom who says yes to everything for our family. Instead, we can seek the Lord's guidance on how to order our days for our family and serve Him best.

APPLICATION

Friend, I understand how easy it is to fall into the patterns of the world and strive hard to build a picture-perfect family that is involved in all the extracurricular activities. I also know the desire to raise a family that is committed to a local church, but somehow become overwhelmed by always doing and never resting in God's presence.

Today, you contrasted the difference between a heart that seeks to honor God and one that is more focused on doing things for the attention and accolades.

As you close out your day, take some time for self-reflection and answer the questions below.

† Do you place more significance on your kids' success or who they are becoming in Christ?

_____

_____

_____

_____

† Some mom's want their kids to have and do things they weren't able to do growing up. While others get swept up in all the activities because that is what all their friends are doing. Can you relate with either or both of these examples? Journal your thoughts below.

_____

_____

_____

_____

Day 1: Choosing a Lighter Burden

✝ How do you measure your success as a mom?

Heavenly Father, in Your Word, You tell me that I am to love You with all my heart, mind, and soul. My greatest calling as a mom, wife, and Your daughter is to share Your love with others at home and wherever I go. When I fall into the patterns of the world's standards of success, remind me of Your greatest commandment to love You and love others. In Jesus's name, amen.

DAY 2

Remembering We Are Known and Held by God

📖 A NOTE FROM LIFE

Years ago, I experienced a health crisis while on vacation that required me to be airlifted to a hospital in my hometown. Before the helicopter arrived, I said goodbye to my husband and two young children, who faced a long four-hour drive home. I put on a brave face to keep my children from worrying too much, but inside, I was scared to death.

When the life-flight team arrived, I was transferred to their stretcher, placed on their monitors, and wheeled out to the waiting helicopter. My heart hurt physically from my health issues but also from worry about my future and the safety of my family, who were driving home.

While aspects of the transfer are foggy, I will never forget the calming presence of the Lord. As the helicopter lifted into the dark sky, I looked out the window and saw lights from towns below and patches of dark countryside. I noticed the string of headlights illuminating the interstate below and knew one of those trucks on the interstate could be my family.

I anxiously prayed for their safety and God's healing hand on my heart. Through the whirring and rumbling of the blades above me, I sensed God's gentle Holy Spirit speak to my soul as if to say, *"Mary, I've got you, my child. I know your worries and fears, and I'm carrying you home in the palm of my hand while leading your family safely home."* I rested comfortably for the rest of the flight, trusting that we would all be okay.

Day 2: Remembering We Are Known and Held by God

 SCRIPTURE STUDY

Before we begin our study today, take a few minutes to read Psalm 139 in your Bible and underline any phrases that stand out to you. Keep your Bible open to Psalm 139 because you will refer back to several passages during your study today.

Throughout his life, David faced difficult seasons of heartache, adversity, and the threat of death. In our reading today, David cried out to God as he sought God's presence in his time of need through his meditation on God's omniscience (all-knowing), omnipresence (always present), and omnipotence (all-powerful) attributes. These attributes of God can be challenging to comprehend, but studying this passage will provide greater insight into these concepts.

Today's study will begin with God's omniscience or all-knowing attribute.

✝ Read Psalm 139:1-5 in your Bible and list the phrases that refer to God knowing us in the space below.

_____

_____

_____

_____

These verses remind us just how deeply the Lord knows each one of us. He has diligently studied and searched us and knows our daily actions intimately and completely. The Lord even knows what is on our hearts before we utter a word. And in our time of need, He surrounds us and lays His hand of security upon us. How amazing is it that God knows the smallest, everyday aspects of our lives!

Come to Me

Friend, rest in the truth that God sees you! God knows you! God cares for you!

✝ How does the realization that the Lord knows you so intimately make you feel?

_____

_____

_____

_____

Let's now study God's omnipresence or always present attribute.

✝ Read Psalm 139:7-12 in your Bible and Romans 8:35-39 below. List (from Psalm 139:7-12) and highlight the phrases (from Romans 8:35-39) that refer to the Lord always being with us.

"Who shall separate us from the love of Christ? Shall tribulation, distress, or persecution, or famine, or nakedness, or danger, or sword? As it is written, 'For your sake we are being killed all the day long; we are regarded as sheep to be slaughtered.' No, in all these things we are more than conquerors through him who loved us. For I am sure that neither death nor life, nor angels nor rulers, nor things present nor things to come, nor powers, nor height nor depth, nor anything else in all creation, will be able to separate us from the love of God in Christ Jesus our Lord." (Romans 8:35-39)

_____

_____

Day 2: Remembering We Are Known and Held by God

___

___

___

___

Our Heavenly Father is always with us. No matter where we go, what we do, or what happens to us, we are never far from His protective presence. And when darkness threatens to overwhelm us, we can trust that we will be okay because He is with us.

✝ How does knowing that you are never far from the Lord's presence comfort you?

___

___

___

___

And finally, let's examine God's omnipotence or all-powerful attribute.

✝ Read Psalm 139:13-16 in your Bible and Ephesians 2:10 below. List (from Psalm 139:13-16) and highlight the phrases (from Ephesians 2:10) that refer to the Lord as our Creator.

"For we are his workmanship, created in Christ Jesus for good works, which God prepared beforehand, that we should walk in them." (Ephesians 2:10)

___

___

Come to Me

_____

_____

_____

_____

Just as God knew every detail of David's life, He also knew every detail of our life from beginning to end. God saw our unformed substance from the moment of conception and had a plan for our life as He intricately knit us together in our mother's womb. When we feel unseen and unloved, we can rest in the comfort of knowing that God loves every aspect of who we are because he "… knit [us] together in [our] mother's womb …" (Psalm 139:13) and breathed life into us (Genesis 2:7).

✝ How does knowing God created and is familiar with every aspect of who you are strengthen you?

_____

_____

_____

_____

Thankfully, my health crisis ended without major complications. As my husband and I processed the events, we were amazed by the Lord's personal comforting presence for each of us. Our Heavenly Father calmed us both as He reminded us that He knew the worry and fear we faced and that just as He had the power to create me with His hands, He also had the healing power I needed.

🙏 APPLICATION

David closes out Psalm 139 with, "Search me, O God, and know my heart! Try me and know my thoughts! And see if there be any grievous way in me, and lead me in the way everlasting!" (vv. 23-24). In these verses, David asks God to search him and know his heart because he finds security in being fully known by God.

Friend, when we face trials and heartache in life, we can easily forget that God, who is all-knowing, always present, and the all-powerful Creator, cares about us. Remember, He holds you in the palm of His hand and wants to come alongside you and lighten the heavy burden you carry.

✝ Journal below how you need to experience one of today's attributes of God.

___

___

___

___

___

___

___

Heavenly Father, thank You for reminding me that You know me intimately. Give me the strength to lay my burdens before You and trust that You will work powerfully according to Your will. In Jesus's name, amen.

DAY 3

Building the Strength to Cast Our Burdens

📖 A NOTE FROM LIFE

My son once worked lifting heavy bags of feed and hay bales daily. He struggled to lift the heavy items when he first started work. But, over time, he learned to use his whole body as he threw the bags and bales with both hands onto pallets. With each repetition, he grew stronger and found it easier to transfer the heavy loads.

📖 SCRIPTURE STUDY

† As we start today's study, read 1 Peter 5:6-7 below and highlight words or phrases that stand out.

> "Humble yourselves, therefore, under the mighty hand of God so that at the proper time he may exalt you, casting all your anxieties on him, because he cares for you." (1 Peter 5:6-7)

Peter urges us to cast our anxieties on the Lord. The Greek word for "casting," *erirpto*, refers to "throwing something upon something else," not simply laying it down. We're encouraged to throw our anxieties and concerns actively and energetically upon the Lord. But, when we've held onto them for so long, the weight of the burdens multiply, and we wonder if we have the strength to cast them upon the Lord. Society would like us to believe that casting off or releasing burdens is a sign of weakness or a character flaw of laziness. However, as David Guzick notes below, releasing burdens takes greater faith and strength to trust God's ability to carry our worries and concerns.

In his commentary on 1 Peter 5:6-7, David Guzick shares a thought and quote from theologian Charles Spurgeon, "This work of casting can be so difficult that we need to use two hands to do it: the hand of prayer and the hand of faith. 'Prayer tells God what the care is, and asks God to help, while faith believes that God can and will do it.'"[vi]

✝ Do you trust and believe that God will help you with your cares and concerns? Are there some concerns that are easier to trust God with?

_____

_____

_____

_____

_____

✝ Look up and read Matthew 6:25-34. In this portion of Jesus's Sermon on the Mount, what did He tell us to do in times of worry?

_____

_____

_____

_____

_____

† How do you seek God in your time of need?

_____
_____
_____

† Read Isaiah 53:4-5 below and circle the words Isaiah prophesied that Jesus would experience on our behalf.

> "Surely he has borne our griefs and carried our sorrows; yet we esteemed him stricken, smitten by God, and afflicted. But he was pierced for our transgressions; he was crushed for our iniquities; upon him was the chastisement that brought us peace, and with his wounds we are healed." (Isaiah 53:4-5)

Isaiah prophesied that God loved us so much that He was willing to send His Son, Jesus, to take on our grief and sorrow. The Greek word for "grief," *holi*, refers to "sickness" and the word for "sorrow," *mak'ob*, speaks to "mental pain." Not only did Jesus come to rescue us from a life of sin, but He also came to carry our burdens upon His shoulders, which weigh us down physically and mentally.

† Read Psalm 55:22 below. What does David tell us the Lord will do when we cast our burdens upon Him?

> "Cast your burden on the LORD, and he will sustain you; he will never permit the righteous to be moved."(Psalm 55:22)

_____
_____
_____

Just as my son needed to learn how to use both hands and his whole body to throw the heavy bags and bales, sometimes it takes more than simply laying down our concerns to the Lord. But how do we cast our burdens when we are so weak? We start with the lighter load and build strength to release the heavier burdens upon the Lord.

APPLICATION

Today, you begin building your strength to fully release your burdens upon the Lord and develop the faith to believe He will work in your life. I hope you are in a quiet space by yourself, but if not, imagine that you are and follow along with me. Open your hands before you and pray the following to the Lord. As you pray and share the worries of your heart, lift your hands to signify that you are casting your prayer upon the Lord.

Heavenly Father, in Your Word, You tell me that as I cast my burdens upon You, Your mighty hand will sustain me (Psalm 55:22). At this moment, Lord, I lift my hands and cast my burden of _____

_____

_____

_____

_____ .

Just as the father cried out, "I believe; help my unbelief!" (Mark 9:24), Lord, I believe that You hear the cry of my heart. I know and trust you are walking with me in this challenging season. Help me feel your presence, carrying me and sustaining me. In Jesus's name, amen.

Friend, this is just the beginning of learning to release your burdens to the Lord. You've carried the world's weight on your shoulders far too long.

✝ As you close out your time with the Lord today, journal how it felt to begin releasing the lighter load of your concerns and worries.

_____

_____

_____

_____

_____

_____

DAY 4

Approaching the Throne of Grace with Honesty

📖 A NOTE FROM LIFE

"God, I don't understand what you're doing!" I sobbed as my fist punched the ceiling of my car, and a guttural cry erupted from the deepest part of my being. I struggled to see through the storm raging outside my car window, which matched the intensity of the storm our family battled.

Several weeks earlier, my husband's parents both experienced life-threatening illnesses within a week of each other. With the answer of a late-night phone call, our calm life as a family of three with a baby on the way was tossed about like a ship on a raging sea. Suddenly, we were balancing our own family needs with bedside vigils at multiple hospitals throughout the state. As we struggled to face the reality that one or both of my husband's parents might not live to meet their new granddaughter.

That night, as I drove home from the hospital, the stress, heartache, and questions erupted from my soul. I questioned God. I yelled at God. And I sobbed tears of sorrow. I desperately wanted answers and for God to miraculously heal Charlie and Harriet. But at that moment, more than answers, I needed God's presence, strength, and endurance. In anguish, I released the burden of everything that weighed me down.

SCRIPTURE STUDY

Friend, I know you carry heavy burdens and need the Lord to come alongside you to lighten your load. If you're like me, you struggle with whether it's okay to be completely honest with the Lord. I want to start today by assuring you that you can honestly come to God's throne of grace in prayer because nothing is hidden from Him. And not just that, but you have the Great High Priest of Jesus, the Son of God, who can sympathize with you (Hebrews 4:13-16). Matthew 6:8b tells us that "…[our] Father knows what [we] need before[we] ask him."

So, today, take a step forward and continue to learn how to cast your burdens upon the Lord. Let Him come alongside you with His yoke to sustain and comfort you as He lightens your load. Psalm 55:1-23 gives an example of David crying out in prayer as he casts his burdens upon God.

† Read Psalm 55:1-23 in your Bible and fill in the chart below. I've given you an example for each one.

David's cries and requests to God	David's expressions of his despair	God's response
vs. 1 David asked God to give an ear to his prayer and plea for mercy	vs. 4 David's heart was in anguish, and he experienced the terrors of death	vs. 16 The Lord will save David

Day 4: Approaching the Throne of Grace with Honesty

✝ Look back over David's expressions of despair. Which of these resonates with you? What other feelings have you experienced in seasons of despair?

_____

_____

_____

_____

Come to Me

David confessed that if he could, he would "...fly away and be at rest..." or "...would wander far away..." and "...lodge in the wilderness ... [and] find a shelter from the raging wind and tempest" (Psalm 55:6-8). I must confess, too, that there have been times when I've desired to run away from the storms that rage around me. But, like David in Psalm 55:16, I call to God, and He gives me peace even amid the storm. And friend, He will give you peace, too, as you call out to God in prayer.

✝ According to Psalm 55:17, when does David cry out to God?

_____

_____

_____

_____

✝ Read Daniel 6:10 in your Bible. We see a similar pattern of prayer when an edict is declared that everyone must pray only to King Darius of the Persian Empire. How often and to whom does Daniel pray?

_____

_____

_____

_____

✝ Read 1 Thessalonians 5:16-18 in your Bible. How often and why does the Apostle Paul say we should pray?

_____

_____

_____

Day 4: Approaching the Throne of Grace with Honesty

We've examined just a few examples of prayer found throughout the Bible in these passages. The point is to understand that prayer is not a one-and-done action first thing in the morning. We can stop and pray any time, day or night.

Before we close out the day, let's take a few minutes to study Psalm 91 as we seek God as our refuge and fortress.

Read Psalm 91 in your Bible. What does God promise to His children who…

✝ Dwell in the shelter of the Most High. Read Psalm 91:1-5.

_____

_____

✝ Make the Lord their dwelling place. Read Psalm 91:9-11.

_____

_____

✝ Hold fast to God in love and know His name. Read Psalm 91:14.

_____

_____

✝ Call to God. Read Psalm 91:15-16.

_____

_____

The night my heart broke open before God, I desperately needed to feel His presence, strength, and endurance. After returning home, I nestled under the covers and listened to the gentle rain on the windowpane. Just as the storm calmed outside, my heart began to feel peaceful as I sensed God lovingly come alongside me and take my stress, heartache, and questions upon His shoulders.

APPLICATION

Friend, we aren't promised an easy, carefree life, but the Lord promises He will be with us through whatever struggles we face or burdens we carry. When we call out to God, dwell in His Word, and hold fast to His love, He will protect us from the storm raging around us. And He will provide the strength we need to keep moving forward in our weakness.

Today, you took another step forward in learning to cast your burdens upon the Lord and allowing Him to come alongside you with His yoke to sustain and comfort you as He lightens your load.

✝ In the space provided, journal your feelings and what you need from the Lord as you release the burdens that weigh you down.

_____

_____

_____

_____

_____

Heavenly Father, thank You for helping me understand that I can be completely honest with You about my feelings. Thank You for loving me unconditionally and taking on the ugliest parts of me that I'm afraid to share with You. Help me feel Your loving arms gently carry me as I trust You in this storm. In Jesus's name, amen.

DAY 5

Review and Reflect

Heavenly Father, thank You for continuing to reveal yourself to me as I study Your Word and learn how to take Your yoke upon my shoulders. Thank You for knowing me so intimately that I can honestly share my struggles and fears with You. Strengthen my heart of faith as I cast my burdens upon You. In Jesus's name, amen.

How was your week studying what it truly means to take the Lord's yoke upon your shoulders? Today, you review what you've learned this week and reflect on how you experienced the Lord's presence.

✝ On day one, you studied God's Word and learned that He wants you to live a life free from striving and rest in who He has called you to be.

✝ On day two, you were reminded that when you face trials and heartache in life, God, who is omniscient (all-knowing), omnipresent (always present), and omnipotent (all-powerful), cares about you. He holds you in the palm of His hand and wants to come alongside you and lighten the heavy burden you carry.

✝ On day three, you learned that casting your burdens upon the Lord isn't just laying them down but throwing them upon Him. As you pray and cast your burdens before the Lord, you strengthen your faith muscles and believe that He will carry your heavy load.

✝ On day four, you took another step forward in laying your burdens upon the Lord. You learned that it's okay to be completely honest with Him because nothing is hidden from Him, and that you have a Great High Priest in Jesus who can sympathize with you.

APPLICATION

Take a few minutes to review how the Lord spoke to you each day. Write out the passage that spoke to your heart this week.

_____
_____
_____
_____
_____

✝ Journal a prayer to the Lord based on the passage above.

_____
_____
_____
_____
_____

✝ Review your daily application questions and journal how the Lord has shepherded and drawn near to you as you've begun to release your burdens to Him.

_____
_____
_____
_____
_____

WEEK 3

Learn from Me

Welcome to week three. I am so glad you are still with me on this journey to find rest for your soul through Jesus. In Matthew 11:29, Jesus tells the disciples, "… learn from me, for I am gentle and lowly in heart." The Greek word for "learn" is *manthano*, and refers to genuinely understanding and accepting a teaching to the point that it becomes a lifelong habit. Jesus describes Himself as gentle and lowly. This description gives a picture of humbleness in relation to God and power under the control of God's Spirit. Jesus desired to show the disciples how to live in the peace of His gentleness and Servant's heart.

For some, it may be challenging to submit to teaching due to negative experiences with uncaring, heavy-handed, or self-important teachers. But Jesus desires to teach from a place of love and humility. Through your study this week, you will gain a deeper understanding of Jesus's character and begin to experience the rest that comes through Him as you live by His example.

As you begin your study today, review your focal passage and open the week in prayer.

✝ Review your favorite translation of Matthew 11:28-30 from day one and write it below.

_____

_____

Come to Me

Heavenly Father, You gently tell me in Your Word to come to You so that You can give rest to my weary and burdened soul. Through this journey, I am learning to open my tightly clenched fists and cast my grief, worry, anxiety, and fear before You so that You can come alongside me and carry my burdens. As I study Your Word this week, give me a heart and mind that sees Your strength, gentleness, and sovereignty. Help me learn more about Your character as I gain a deeper trust in You. In Jesus's name, amen.

DAY 1

Learning from Jesus's Examples

📖 A NOTE FROM LIFE

"Mary, has anyone told you that you have more problems than Carter has peanuts?"

Those words stung deep inside my 17-year-old body as a teacher berated me for falling grades in front of a full classroom. (For those who are too young to remember, Jimmy Carter, our thirty-ninth president, was a peanut farmer from Georgia.)

Fast-forward a year, and a professor in college quietly pulled me aside after class and gently asked, "Mary, is everything okay? I've noticed your grades are slipping, and you don't seem to be yourself. What can I do to help you?"

In my late teens and early twenties, years of family strife came to a head when my parents divorced. My grades suffered and my attitude was like a rollercoaster as I struggled to cope with the many emotions I experienced as we navigated the upheaval of our family. I don't know what these two teachers faced in their personal lives, but I do know they responded in completely different ways to the outward signs of the inner angst I was facing.

There may be times, even during your own struggles, that you need to reach out and help someone else. In your study today, you will learn how Jesus, while facing His own struggles, humbly served His disciples and set an example for them about how to serve and care for others.

SCRIPTURE STUDY

† Read John 13:1-17 and underline the words or phrases that stand out to you.

_____

_____

_____

_____

† Briefly summarize John 13:1-17 in the space provided.

_____

_____

_____

_____

Jesus knew He was partaking in His last meal with the disciples before Judas's betrayal, which would lead to His arrest and death. In those last few hours, He chose to display the heart of a servant and wash the disciples' feet. But Simon Peter questioned Jesus because he couldn't understand why Jesus would perform such a lowly act.

† Go back and read John 13:6-8 again. Summarize the interaction between Jesus and Simon Peter in the space below.

_____

_____

_____

_____

Day 1: Learning from Jesus's Examples

I love how Jesus responded, "What I am doing you do not understand now, but afterward you will understand" (John 13:7). Jesus continued to wash Simon Peter's feet along with the rest of the disciples' feet. This act signified Jesus washing away their sin, but Jesus also wanted them to learn another lesson.

✝ Read John 13:12-17 again. What lesson did Jesus want them to learn?

___

___

___

___

Jesus used this intimate time with the disciples as an opportunity to model how they should serve one another and those they encounter throughout their journeys.

✝ Look up 1 Peter 2:18-25 ESV and fill in the blanks below.

"Servants, be subject to your masters _____,

not only to _____ but also to the unjust.

For this is _____, when, mindful of God,

_____ while suffering unjustly. For what

credit is it if, _____, you endure? But if

when you _____, this is a gracious thing

in the sight of God. For to this you have been called, because

_____, leaving you an example, so that

you might follow in his steps. He _____,

63

neither was deceit found in his mouth. When he was reviled, he _____; when _____, he did not threaten, but continued _____ justly. He himself _____ on the tree, that we _____. By his wounds _____. For you were straying like sheep, but _____ to the Shepherd and Overseer of your souls."

✝ What does Peter say is gracious in the sight of God?

_____

_____

_____

_____

✝ Read the above passage again, underline Jesus's suffering, and circle His response to that suffering.

✝ As you study Jesus's example, how are you following His steps in your struggles?

_____

_____

_____

_____

Day 1: Learning from Jesus's Examples

We don't always understand why things happen, but we can trust that our Lord and Savior knows and understands our struggles. He has experienced grief, betrayal, and the ultimate sacrifice of death for each of us. He is our example of trusting God's ultimate plan and how we should respond to others as we follow Him.

Throughout this week, you will continue to study and learn about God's character. Before you close out day one, briefly examine other passages that teach about God's character.

✝ Look up the following passages and draw a line to match the character of God with the corresponding passage.

Matthew 10:29-31	humble
Joshua 1:6-9	sovereignty
Psalm 144:1-2	gentleness/comfort
Isaiah 40:11	nearness in our struggles
Psalm 86:15	courage
Psalm 34:18	rock
Philippians 2:5-8	steadfast love

APPLICATION

The behavior of my teachers reveals opposite responses to someone facing personal struggles—how to come alongside them and how not to respond. As you studied today's passages, you learned how Jesus humbly served His disciples and set an example for how to serve and care for others as you follow His steps in your time of need. Over the next few days, you will continue to study the character of God.

† Reflect on a time when you were called upon to serve someone in their time of need while continuing to manage your own responsibilities and hard struggles. In the space provided, reflect on your response to the situation. If you look back on the time and realize you could've handled things differently, is there someone who is a good example of how to serve others while going through their own difficulties? Share some of the lessons you can learn from their example.

___

___

___

___

___

___

___

___

___

___

✝ Write out a prayer using the scripture passage above of the character trait of God that you need to learn or experience most.

Heavenly Father, thank You for giving me Your Holy Word, which teaches me how to humbly serve others, even as I face my own struggles. Give me a heart that loves others as Jesus loved. In Jesus's name, amen.

DAY 2

Finding Comfort and Rest in the Gentleness of God

📖 A NOTE FROM LIFE

On July 3rd our son Garrett entered the world with a bang through an emergency c-section after his heart stopped during labor. For the next 24 hours, I faded in and out of sleep as I battled severe nausea and the effects of eclampsia. I remember waking to the sound of thunder and rain hitting the window. Through the fog of medication, I looked over and saw the most beautiful sight. While the storm raged outside, my husband gently cradled our newborn son in his arms. Garrett slept peacefully, enveloped in his daddy's gentle, protective arms.

Later, as I recalled the difficult circumstances of Garrett's birth and remembered the way my husband held him in his arms, the Holy Spirit whispered to my soul: *Not only was Garrett cradled in the arms of his earthly father during a storm, but he was also held in his Heavenly Father's hands during the dangers of his birth.* This gives me the peace I need to know that I am carried when life's burdens weigh me down.

Friend, I wonder if you, too, need to experience the peace that comes as the Lord gently cradles you in His loving arms. Join me today as you continue to learn from the Lord and find comfort and rest in His gentle, caring nature.

Day 2: Finding Comfort and Rest in the Gentleness of God

 SCRIPTURE STUDY

✝ Look up Isaiah 40:11 in your Bible and write it below. Underline any words or phrases that stand out to you.

_____

_____

_____

_____

In this passage, Isaiah speaks to God as a Shepherd who gently gathers His flock and cares for them. In his commentary, David Guzik notes, "He doesn't cast the weak lambs over His shoulder, as a shepherd might carry a sheep. Instead, He lovingly cradles them in His bosom, close to His heart. That is both a safe place and a tender place."[vii]

In Psalm 23, David also describes the Lord as a protective shepherd who provides rest. Look up Psalm 23 and fill in the blanks below to learn how to find rest in the Lord during life's burdens.

"The Lord is my shepherd; I shall not want. He _____ in green pastures. He _____ beside still waters. He _____ my soul. He _____ in paths of righteousness for his name's sake. Even though I walk through the valley of the shadow of death, I will fear no evil, for _____; your rod and your staff, they _____. You _____ before me in the presence of my enemies; you _____ with oil; my cup overflows. Surely goodness and mercy shall follow me all the days of my life, and I shall dwell in the house of the LORD forever."

Come to Me

✝ Take a few moments to read back over Isaiah 40:11 and Psalm 23. List the action verbs you read in both passages in the space below.

___

Our Heavenly Father isn't passive in His care for us. When we are weak and struggling, He gathers us in His arms and gently leads us to rest, where we can be comforted and restored.

One of my favorite life verses is Isaiah 40:29-31, "He gives power to the faint, and to him who has no might he increases strength. Even youths shall faint and be weary, and young men shall fall exhausted; but they who wait for the Lord shall renew their strength; they shall mount up with wings like eagles; they shall run and not be weary; they shall walk and not faint."

There will come a time when we are overwhelmed and exhausted. In our weakness, we can look to God, who will give us the strength we need as we submit and wait for Him to gently care for us.

✝ How do you need to find comfort and rest in the Lord in your current season?

___

Before closing out the day, take a few moments to read Psalm 86 in your Bible and highlight any words or phrases that stand out to you.

Psalm 86 is known as a Prayer of David. We don't know the specific time in his life when David wrote the Psalm, nor do we know the exact source of his trouble. However, through this prayer, David demonstrates how to ask God for help while thanking Him for His steadfast love.

✝ Read the passages below and underline the descriptions that David used to express gratitude to God for his character.

"For you, O Lord, are good and forgiving, abounding in steadfast love to all who call upon you." (Psalm 86:5)

"For great is your steadfast love toward me; you have delivered my soul from the depths of Sheol." (Psalm 86:13)

"But you, O Lord, are a God merciful and gracious, slow to anger and abounding in steadfast love and faithfulness." (Psalm 86:15)

In these three passages and throughout Psalm 86, David expressed gratitude to God for His goodness, forgiveness, mercy, grace, patience, and steadfast love. The Hebrew word for steadfast love is *hesed*, which expresses "God's abundant loving kindness and compassion."[viii]

Throughout David's life, the Lord faithfully answered David's cries for help, so he knew he could go to the Lord again. Not only did he desire to be rescued, but he also desired to know God completely and live out His truth. We see this when he asked, "Teach me your way, O LORD, that I may walk in your truth; unite my heart to fear your name" (Psalm 86:11). David knew he could only have a united heart with the Lord when he fully submitted and learned from the Lord.

Friend, as we release our burdens before the Lord and trust Him to walk with us every step, may we also pray to submit and learn from Him.

APPLICATION

I remember my husband tenderly cradling our newborn son in his arms during the storm. When life's storms surround us, our Heavenly Father gathers us in His comforting arms and protects us in our most vulnerable and defenseless moments. I can't help but think about being held so close to my Heavenly Father that I can hear His heartbeat. The thought of this brings me comfort when I'm overwhelmed by life's burdens.

✝ What emotions or thoughts go through your mind as you think of being so close to your Heavenly Father during the storms of life that you can hear His heartbeat?

_____

_____

_____

_____

_____

Heavenly Father, thank You for Your steadfast, gentle love. You know the struggle I face in releasing control over to You in the storms of life. Give me the strength I need to release control so that I may rest in Your gentle embrace and receive Your rest and comfort. In Jesus's name, amen.

DAY 3

Drawing Courage from God's Sovereignty

📖 A NOTE FROM LIFE

On my writing desk, I have a smooth stone placed where I can see it anytime doubt and discouragement begin to take hold. On one side, the phrase "Not today, Satan, GOD has already WON!!!" is written in black permanent marker. On the other side, I'm reminded to take courage in God's constant presence when I read Joshua 1:9, "Be strong and courageous. Do not be terrified; do not be discouraged, for the Lord your God will be with you wherever you go."

One of the things I struggle with the most when I'm overwhelmed by life's burdens is feeling like I'm completely alone and that God doesn't know what I'm going through, or even worse, doesn't care. Friend, I wonder if you feel the same way.

Today, we examine scripture which encourages us to know that God, in His sovereignty, attends to the details of our lives. As we begin to trust Him as our Rock and Protector, we will have the courage to face any battle that comes our way, knowing He is by our side.

SCRIPTURE STUDY

In Matthew 10:6-7, Jesus called and sent the twelve Apostles "...to the lost sheep of the house of Israel..." to proclaim that "... the kingdom of heaven is at hand." As He gave instructions, He also warned them of persecution and hatred. But in Matthew 10:26-31, Jesus encouraged them not to fear.

✝ Read Matthew 10:26-31 in your Bible. Highlight the words or phrases that stand out to you.

✝ In Matthew 10:26-31, why did Jesus tell the Apostles not to fear?

_____

_____

_____

_____

The Apostles were more valuable to God than two tiny sparrows sold for the smallest coin in Roman currency. Jesus told the disciples that all the hairs on their heads were numbered. If He knows everything about the disciples and is concerned with the tiniest detail, why should we think He doesn't feel the same way about us?

✝ Look up Job 42:1-6 ESV. Highlight the words and phrases that stand out to you.

✝ Fill in the blanks in the verses below from Job 42:2-5 ESV:

"I know that you can _____, and that _____ of yours can be _____." (vs. 2)

Day 3: Drawing Courage from God's Sovereignty

"'Who is this that hides counsel without knowledge?' Therefore I have _____, things too _____." (vs. 3)

"I had _____ by the _____, but _____;" (vs. 5)

Job had experienced the most devastating crisis imaginable: the loss of so many that he loved, everything he owned, and his health. But in this passage, he admits that he once intellectually knew of God and trusted that He could do everything. Now, even though he couldn't fully understand God's plans, Job had experienced God's presence and had a deeper knowledge and understanding of God. Through his crisis, Job moved from head knowledge to heart knowledge.

✝ Reflect on a time of need in your life. Did you sense God's presence then? If not, do you now see how God provided for and shepherded you through that need? Perhaps discussing the time with someone close to you can help you see God's presence even more clearly. How does the awareness of God's presence in your life help you know Him better?

_____

_____

_____

_____

As you learn to trust God's sovereignty in your life, you can also lean on Him as your Rock and Protector. King David praises God in Psalm 144 for being his source of help in battle.

✝ Look up Psalm 144:1-2 in the ESV translation and write the passage in the space provided below.

_____

_____

_____

_____

✝ Circle each name or title for God that David used to express how he had experienced God's character.

David knew and experienced God as each of these personally. God prepared and trained David for battle during his years in the fields as he cared for and protected the sheep from wolves and other dangers. God also protected David from the threat of King Saul and others who sought to kill him.

Before you close out your day, take a few minutes to study the courage God gives you to face any battle that comes your way with Him by your side.

Read Joshua 1:5-9 below.

> "No man shall be able to stand before you all the days of your life. Just as I was with Moses, so I will be with you. I will not leave you or forsake you. Be strong and courageous, for you shall cause this people to inherit the land that I swore to their fathers to give them. Only be strong and very courageous, being careful to do according to all the law that Moses my servant commanded you. Do not turn from it to the right hand or to the left, that you may have good success wherever you go. This Book of the Law shall not depart from your mouth, but you shall meditate on it day and night, so that you may be careful to do according to all that is written in it. For then you will make your way prosperous, and

then you will have good success. Have I not commanded you? Be strong and courageous. Do not be frightened, and do not be dismayed, for the LORD your God is with you wherever you go."

God told Joshua that he must do three things as he faced the challenges of leading the Israelites into and taking possession of the Promised Land.

✝ In Joshua 1:5-9, circle the phrases that reference God's presence being with Joshua.

✝ Underline the phrases referencing strength and courage.

✝ Highlight the phrases that instruct Joshua about the Law of Moses.

✝ What did God say Joshua must do to be successful?

_____

_____

_____

_____

Like Joshua, when we remain in God's Word, He provides us the courage and strength to confront any battle we encounter.

APPLICATION

What a blessing it is to know that when we feel alone in our struggles, God's Word reminds us that He is with us no matter what we face and is ready to give us His courage as we trust Him to be our Rock and Protector.

✝ List ways that you've personally experienced God's work in your life through God's characteristics of sovereignty, our Rock and Protector, and Source of courage.

_____

_____

_____

_____

Heavenly Father, thank You for the reminder of Your presence and sovereignty over my life. When I struggle with doubt and discouragement, remind me that You have already won the battle, and because of that, I can be strong and courageous, no matter what I face. In Jesus's name, amen.

DAY 4

Feeling God's Nearness in Our Time of Need

📖 A NOTE FROM LIFE

I step onto the stage with the rest of the praise team, highlighted by a spotlight, microphone in hand, and a smile, ready to help lead the congregation in worship. Young and old voices weave with the piano, praise band, and orchestra to form a mighty worship chorus. On the outside, I joyfully lift my hand in praise, while on the inside, my heart races, my stomach churns, and the very depth of my soul cries, "Dear God, I am so tired! Make this all go away!" I am weakened by anger and hurt from difficult circumstances in my life, and every ounce of my being wants to escape to the darkest corner of the sanctuary and hide.

As darkness threatens to envelop me in a room filled with voices, I feel alone and so far away from God. I remember two passages my spiritual mentor recently shared: "…God is light; in him, there is no darkness at all" (1 John 1:5 NIV) and "This is how we know that we belong to the truth and how we set our hearts at rest in his presence: If our hearts condemn us, we know that God is greater than our hearts, and he knows everything"(1 John 3:19-20 NIV).

In this moment, when I feel the full weight of my burdens, I recall one of God's most fundamental truths: when I stand in His light, He is with me and will give me the strength I need to stand strong, firm, and secure. When I remain in His truth and trust Him to fight my battles, He will make His truth known. And although my heart is weak from the pain, when I keep my heart focused on Him, He will be the protection I need.

Today, you will study and learn about God's nearness and protection in your time of need.

 SCRIPTURE STUDY

David wrote Psalm 34 from the cave of Adullam, where he hid from King Saul and Abimelech. While hiding in fear, David praised the Lord for His goodness and protection. David used this moment of praise to encourage the other men in the cave. When burdened with worry and fear, we can also use David's psalm as a source of encouragement as we seek to grow closer to the Lord.

✝ Read Psalm 34. In the space provided, list David's actions of praise.

_____

_____

_____

_____

✝ List the evidence of God's nearness in Psalm 34:14-22.

_____

_____

_____

_____

In Psalm 34:7, David encouraged, "The angel of the LORD encamps around those who fear him, and delivers them." At his lowest point, David still trusted in God's encompassing protection of the angel of the LORD. We see another example of God's nearness and divine protection in 2 Kings 6:15-17.

✝ Read 2 Kings 6:8-17 in your Bible and underline any words or phrases that stand out to you.

Elisha and his servant fled to the valley of Dothan because they faced the wrath of the Syrian King. Early in the morning, Elisha's servant woke to an army with horses and chariots surrounding the city. Overwhelmed by fear and seeing the obstacles before him, the servant cried to Elisha, "Alas, my master! What shall we do?" (2 Kings 6:15b).

But Elisha had eyes of faith that could see the bigger picture of God's protection and blessing. "He said, 'Do not be afraid, for those who are with us are more than those who are with them.' Then Elisha prayed and said, 'O Lord, please open his eyes that he may see.' So the LORD opened the eyes of the young man, and he saw, and behold, the mountain was full of horses and chariots of fire all around Elisha" (2 Kings 6:16-17).

When overwhelmed with the weight of our burdens, it's easy to forget that the Lord is with us. Our eyes only see the obstacles before us. However, Elisha and David are both examples of men who faced intense peril and still chose to see the blessings and protection God had for them as they viewed their situation through the eyes of faith.

✝ Who are you as you walk through seasons of adversity? Are you the servant who sees the obstacles through the eyes of fear? Or are you David and Elijah, and like them you see with eyes of faith as you praise and trust the Lord in the storm? Or can you relate to all three in different seasons of adversity? In the space provided, write a prayer to the Lord based on who you are in your season of adversity.

_____

_____

_____

_____

_____

_____

_____

Before you close your day, take a few minutes to reflect on Jesus Christ's true act of humility and its meaning for us today.

✝ Read Philippians 2:5-8 below and circle how Jesus displayed humility.

> "Have this mind among yourselves, which is yours in Christ Jesus, who, though he was in the form of God, did not count equality with God a thing to be grasped, but emptied himself by taking the form of a servant, being born in the likeness of men. And being found in human form, he humbled himself by becoming obedient to the point of death, even death on a cross." (Philippians 2:5-8)

✝ Read John 1:1 and John 1:4 below and underline any noteworthy words or phrases.

> "In the beginning was the Word, and the Word was with God, and the Word was God." (John 1:1)

> "And the Word became flesh and dwelt among us, and we have seen his glory, glory as of the only Son from the Father, full of grace and truth." (John 1:4)

Friend, I don't want you to miss the significance of these passages. Jesus—God in human form—didn't have to humble Himself and experience the realities of a fallen world, but He did, coming as near to you and me as He could without sinning. And He did that so that we could find comfort in knowing He sees us and has experienced the things that burden us. Jesus knows what it feels like to be betrayed by a trusted friend (Matthew 26:47-50). Jesus understands the grief of losing a loved one (John 11:32-36). And He understands the effects of being in a wilderness season (Luke 4:1-2).

Jesus was the Word, and the Word was God. He emptied Himself of His own interests and took on the form of a man. And in humble obedience, he suffered the cruelest form of punishment reserved for the worst criminals and experienced excruciating torture and agony to take on our burdens and sins.

And when it seemed like hope was lost, Jesus promised our Heavenly Father would "…give you another advocate to help you and be with you forever—the Spirit of truth," who "…lives with you and will be with you" (John 14:16-17).

✝ Read John 14:25-27. What will the Holy Spirit do for us?

_____

_____

_____

_____

Not only does God know our thoughts, but we are also given a channel (the Holy Spirit) for perceiving some of His thoughts as they pertain to our daily lives and experiences. That is a profound nearness. And through that nearness, we have the peace of God that settles our souls when our hearts are troubled and afraid (John 14:27).

APPLICATION

I felt utterly alone as I stood on the stage that Sunday morning. However, I am deeply thankful for the gift of the Holy Spirit, which reminded me of God's nearness during my time of need. And friend, you are not alone either. As a child of God, you have been given the Holy Spirit, who speaks truth to your heart and provides the peace you need.

✝ How do you need to experience God's nearness in your current struggle?

_____

_____

_____

_____

_____

_____

Heavenly Father, thank You for loving me so much that You sent Your Son to earth to take my burdens and sins upon Himself. And thank You for the gift of the Holy Spirit, who is with me and provides the comfort and peace I need when life is heavy. Give me the strength I need to lay my burdens down so that I can fully experience Your nearness. In Jesus's name, amen.

DAY 5

Review and Reflect

Heavenly Father, thank You for setting an example for me in the life of Jesus as to how to serve and care for others. And thank You for displaying Your character and revealing the truth that I am never alone, because I have the gift of Your Holy Spirit's presence. In Jesus's name, amen.

Congratulations, my friend! You've come to the end of week three. That means you have one more week on your journey to find rest for your soul. I pray that as you've studied and learned from the character of your Heavenly Father, you have been able to trust Him more and have begun to release the burdens that weigh you down and allow Him to carry them for you.

Let's review what you learned about God's character this week.

† On day one, you learned that while Jesus faced His own struggles, He humbly served His disciples and set an example for them on how to serve and care for others.

† On day two, you continued to learn from the Lord and find comfort and rest in His gentle, caring nature as you learned to submit to Him.

† On day three, you examined scripture that helped you understand that God, in His Sovereignty, knows and shepherds the smallest details of your life. As you trust Him as your Rock and Protector, you'll find the courage to face any battle that comes your way with Him.

✝ On day four, you learned of God's nearness in your struggles through the gift of the Holy Spirit and began to understand the depths of God's love for you and Jesus's desire to take your burdens and sins upon Himself.

APPLICATION

Take a few minutes to review how the Lord spoke to you each day. Write out the passage that stood out to you this week.

_____
_____
_____
_____

✝ Journal a prayer to the Lord based on the passage above.

_____
_____
_____
_____

✝ Review your closing prayers each day and journal how the Lord has met you as you continue to release your burdens to Him.

_____
_____
_____
_____

WEEK 4

Find Rest for Your Soul

Welcome to week four, my friend. I'm so thankful you've joined me on this amazing journey as you've answered the Lord's invitation to come to Him, learned to release your burdens to Him, and discovered how to walk in the peace and strength of His character. This week, you will "...find rest for your soul..." because Jesus's "... yoke is easy, and [His] burden is light" (Matthew 11:29-30). The Greek word for "find" is *heurisko*, which is an exclamation of joy as something new is learned. Our English word, "Eureka!" is derived from this word. And as we find rest in Him, we will find the restoration of joy and spiritual rest in Jesus while continuing to live in the reality of life.

Before you begin your last week of study, take a few minutes to record your journey thus far.

✝ Looking back at week one, day one what words did you use to describe rest for your soul? Is there anything you would add to that list?

_____

_____

Come to Me

At the close of week one, day four you imagined sitting at the well with Jesus and sharing with Him what you needed physically, emotionally, and spiritually. Briefly summarize your thoughts and feelings when you started this study.

_____

_____

_____

_____

_____

_____

_____

_____

_____

_____

_____

_____

_____

DAY 1

Trusting the Holy Spirit and Jesus to Intercede for Us

📖 A NOTE FROM LIFE

I stood shaking uncontrollably in the middle of my den floor as the weight of life's burdens crushed my spirit. Two people I loved more than life itself hurt in their own unique way, and I had no idea how to rescue them from their pain. With each of them in separate rooms, my heart was torn in two as I struggled to know which one to help first. I was desperate to fix their problems and desperate to heal their pain.

For weeks, I endured countless sleepless nights, calming fears, explaining reality, and soothing my precious loved ones' anxious heart. As the dark, sleepless nights gave way to the break of day, we put on a brave face to the world, pretending that all was well within our little family. But the truth was that it wasn't well, no matter how hard I tried to calm, explain, and soothe. The added sleep deficit took a toll, causing increased stress and strain on our family, which led to further turmoil. The combination of stress, strain, and exhaustion led to nonexistent coping skills, which eventually brought us to a breaking point. I realized I couldn't fix our family and couldn't be the healing balm we all needed.

Standing in the middle of my den floor, I discovered through my broken, crumbling heart that God was the only One who could bear the weight that threatened to crush us. It was only through Him that we were going to find our way out of those dark days and nights.

Come to Me

As my soul cried out for God's help to bear the burdens we faced, His strong, sweet spirit gently whispered to my soul, "Let me carry this for you. Take those you love by their trembling hands and bring their pain to me." And so, I did. With wordless groans and tears, my heart cried out as I released the tight grip of my heart and fists and placed the concerns of our family at the foot of the cross.

Friend, even when we are at our weakest, exhausted by the weight of grief, anxiety, fear, or worry, we still have hope. We can rest in the assurance of knowing we are more than conquerors through Jesus Christ, who loves us and intercedes for us as He sits at the right hand of our Heavenly Father. And we have the hope and peace found in the Holy Spirit, who goes to our Heavenly Father and translates our wordless groans and tears.

SCRIPTURE STUDY

† Read Romans 8:34-39 in your Bible. Who sits at the right hand of God, interceding for us?

_____

_____

_____

† List below what Paul said could not separate us from the love of Christ. (See Romans 8:35, 38-39)

_____

_____

_____

_____

Day 1: Trusting the Holy Spirit and Jesus to Intercede for Us

What a comfort it is to know that no matter what we face, nothing can separate us from the love of God in Christ Jesus. But Jesus isn't the only One interceding for us in our time of need.

✝ Look up Romans 8:26-27 in the ESV translation and fill in the blanks below.

"Likewise the _____ helps us in our _____.

For we do not know what _____ as we ought, but

the _____ for us with _____.

And he who _____

knows what is the _____, because the

_____ for the _____ according to

the _____."

✝ Read the above passage again and circle what the Spirit does for us.

As you read this passage, notice that "helps" is in the present tense. The Holy Spirit actively helps us with our weaknesses. The Greek word for "help" in this passage refers to "someone helping another carry a heavy load."[ix] When we struggle to find the words to lay our worries and concerns before the Lord, the Holy Spirit intercedes for us and takes our hurt and prayer to the Lord, aligning it with God's will for us.

Paul tells us that for "...those who love God all things work together for good..." (Romans 8:28). This doesn't mean that our lives will always be full of rainbows and sunshine. But, even when the storms of life darken our days, God will use both the good days *and* the bad days to grow us and bring us closer to Him.

✝ In the space provided, reflect on a particularly good season of your life or a particularly bad season. Journal how that season helped you experience God more deeply. For instance, what characteristic of God did you experience in that season?

_____

_____

_____

_____

_____

The hardest thing I've ever done was admitting I couldn't hold my loved ones' lives together. I realized I had to trust God to see them through to the other side—whatever that looked like. I had to trust that His way was best and that He would show us His glory in the end, even if it wasn't what I wanted.

But how, you ask. "How did you trust God? How did you hand it over to Him? You don't know what I'm struggling through. You don't see the pain and heartache I face each day."

You know what? You're right. I don't. But what I do know is God knows.

Psalm 44:21 says, "…He knows the secrets of the heart." Not only does God know, but He cares. He is aware of your pain and your heartache. God sees you crying at night when no one else is there to see you. He hears the wailing of your heart that no one else hears. And I know He sits with you, ready to hold you as you collapse. I know this because I learned that night that when pain, fear, worry, and anger begin to overtake us, we need to release them all to Him and allow Him to carry the heavy load and fight our battles.

APPLICATION

This week, you will continue to find rest for your souls as you allow God to carry your burdens and fight your battles.

✝ Write down what you hold tightly between clenched fists in the space provided. Be honest with yourself and God. It's okay to admit it. God knows what it is. Write it down, speak it out loud, or whisper it within your heart, and then pray this prayer with me.

_____

_____

_____

_____

_____

_____

Heavenly Father, I come broken before You on my knees. You are all-knowing, my Creator and my God. I'm sorry I have held on so tightly to _____. Lord, I realize You are the only One who can bear the weight of what I'm trying to carry. You are the only One who can mend my broken heart and take the pain away. Help me trust that through Christ and the Holy Spirit, I have Someone who will intercede for me when I don't know what to say or do. Thank You for never giving up on me, even when I fail to turn to You. Lord, I ask that You give me the strength to hand control over to You fully so that I may find true rest in You. Give me the strength to daily, moment by moment, keep the eyes of my heart focused on You, not on what is visually in front of me, but on Your light and strength. In Jesus's name, amen.

DAY 2

Fixing Our Eyes on the Eternal Glory of God

📖 A NOTE FROM LIFE

Years ago, my husband had a conversation with our pastor when our family experienced what felt like a series of crushing blows one after another. In a moment of frustration, Jeff told our pastor that he had always heard that God would never give you more than you can handle. Our pastor gently corrected him and said, "I hear you, but you've got your theology wrong. There will be times you *will* experience more than you can handle, but it will never be more than what *God* can carry for you."

I remembered that conversation many years later when job stress for my husband, caring for my mom who was battling terminal cancer, sleepless nights from worry for a hurting child, and betrayal from a trusted friend, all threatened to take me into a pit of depression and anxiety. I recall countless mornings sitting in my worn, brown leather recliner, bathed in the dim glow of a single light, journaling my heart out to God.

I couldn't understand why we were experiencing so much heartache and pain. Truthfully, my flesh wanted to run away from it all because I was completely overwhelmed. But my heart knew that God must have a bigger plan than what I could see in my myopic view. My prayer was that God would somehow give me the strength and endurance to not run away, but to trust Him and look to Him to carry the heartache that threatened to overwhelm me.

I wonder if, like me, you find it hard not to give in to your flight reflex and run away when you are overwhelmed by the hardships of life. If you do, today's passage will help you focus on the eternal perspective in your suffering rather than the temporary perspective so that you can see God's divine plan for His eternal glory.

SCRIPTURE STUDY

✝ Read 2 Corinthians 4:7-10, 16-18 in your Bible. Highlight any words or phrases that stand out to you.

✝ Fill in the blanks below from 2 Corinthians 4:8-9 (NIV).

"We are _____ on every side, but not _____; _____, but not in _____; _____, but not _____; _____, but not _____."

The Apostle Paul was no stranger to suffering and the dangers of life. He knew firsthand the realities of 2 Corinthians 4:8-9.

✝ Read 2 Corinthians 11:23-28 in your Bible and list the forms of suffering that Paul endured.

Paul shared his experience and survival after suffering, knowing it was not to bring himself glory but to bring God glory.

In 2 Corinthians 4:7, Paul states, "…we have this treasure in jars of clay, to show that the surpassing power belongs to God and not to us." Paul used the metaphor, "treasures in jars of clay" to explain that we, as frail and fallible humans, carry the treasure of the gospel of Christ within us.

To understand the concept of "treasures in jars of clay," let's look at the story of Gideon's defeat of the Midianites. Read Judges 7:7-21 in your Bible.

✝ In Judges 7:16, what did Gideon place in the hands of the army?

_____

_____

_____

_____

_____

✝ In Judges 7:19-20, what did the army do with the jars, and what was revealed?

_____

_____

_____

_____

_____

Day 2: Fixing Our Eyes on the Eternal Glory of God

The torches were hidden in clay jars. Once broken, the light from the torches lit the way as the army descended upon the Midian army. The broken jars gave way to the light, leading them to victory.

Within our earthly, fragile vessels resides the treasure of the gospel, which is the light of Jesus Christ. Even though life's hardships and struggles crack our outward layer, we have the hope of knowing that the power of God shines bright in our weaknesses.

† Let's look back at 2 Corinthians 4:16-18 (ESV) once more.

> "So we do not lose heart. Though our outer self is wasting away, our inner self is being renewed day by day. For this light momentary affliction is preparing for us an eternal weight of glory beyond all comparison, as we look not to the things that are seen but to the things that are unseen. For the things that are seen are transient, but the things that are unseen are eternal."

† Why does Paul say we should not lose heart?

† What do our "light and momentary troubles" achieve for us?

† What are we to fix our eyes on and why?

_____

_____

_____

_____

The Greek word Paul uses for "light" affliction is used only one other time. We find it in our focal passage for this study, "For my yoke is easy, and my burden is light" (Matthew 11:30). Our affliction and hardships are light in weight and easy to bear because Jesus takes up our burdens to give us His eternal weight of glory. When we choose to take our focus off the heartache and pain we experience and instead fix our eyes on the eternal glory that lies ahead, our lives shine the light of Christ in our weakness as we experience the true joy found in Him.

Day 2: Fixing Our Eyes on the Eternal Glory of God

🙏 APPLICATION

Friend, I'm going to be honest with you. If I had given in to my flight reflex that I shared with you as we opened the day, you would not be working through this Bible study right now. *Come to Me* was born out of my soul searching and realization that I was broken under the weight of my burdens, and I needed to trust the Lord to carry those burdens. As He put the pieces back together of my cracked vessel, I have been able to share the goodness of God's work in my life with you and others who are hurting.

✝ Journal how you have seen and experienced the Lord's renewal as you've released your burdens to Him.

_____

_____

_____

_____

_____

_____

Heavenly Father, thank You for helping me see that when my outer vessel cracks and feels as if it's wasting away, the reality is that's when others can see Your work in my life. Yes, I may feel overwhelmed and want to run, but I know that You have a divine plan for my life and will use the hard seasons of life to strengthen me so that I can display Your goodness. In Jesus's name, amen.

DAY 3

Regaining Our Strength

📖 A NOTE FROM LIFE

I live in a neighborhood with streetlights and houses that often have porch lights on at night. When my kids were younger, we walked to an open area on our street to watch a meteor shower. Unfortunately, due to the streetlights and ambient light from the houses, we only saw the occasional falling star dimly trail through the night sky.

Several years later, we were at the beach during another meteor shower. Standing on the beach in the darkness, we gazed in awe at the glittering array of stars and constellations that filled the night sky. Our excitement increased each time we caught sight of another meteor blazing overhead.

The contrast between the two meteor showers was stunning. The pollution of the lights created by man dimmed the brilliance of the celestial light created by God. However, when worldly influences were removed, we were able to see God's heavenly host of stars and constellations on bright display.

So it can be in our lives. The light of God within us may appear dim when we opt for the lesser lights of worldly solutions to our problems. When we focus on God above all human wisdom, His light in us shines brighter. When, like the stars, we glorify God in darkness, relying on and praising Him in our troubles, His light shines the brightest, and others can see His glory. Our focal passage for today reminds me of that night and leaves me in awe of God's glory and power.

SCRIPTURE STUDY

Over the last several weeks of studying God's Word, you have begun to experience the peace and rest that comes when you release your burdens to the Lord. In week 2, day 3, you learned how to strengthen your faith muscles to cast your burdens on the Lord. Today, you will learn how to regain the light of your spiritual strength that has been dimmed by the influence of the world as you trust God to sustain you in His strength.

✝ Read Isaiah 40:26-31 in your Bible and underline the words or phrases that stand out to you.

Isaiah 40:26 tells us the Holy One created each star and called them by name. As I ponder this, I am overwhelmed by the greatness of our Heavenly Father, but I am also reminded that just as He knows the name of each star, He created me and knows my name (Isaiah 43:1).

✝ As you think about the greatness of God, how does it make you feel to know He created you and knows you by name?

_____

_____

_____

_____

✝ Read Isaiah 40:28-29 again in your Bible and write the words that speak to God's endurance and wisdom in the space provided.

_____

_____

_____

_____

Come to Me

✝ According to Isaiah 40:29-31, to whom does God give power and strength?

_____

_____

_____

_____

✝ Read the verses below and underline words or phrases that stand out to you.

"Consider it pure joy, my brothers and sisters, whenever you face trials of many kinds, because you know that the testing of your faith produces perseverance. Let perseverance finish its work so that you may be mature and complete, not lacking anything. If any of you lacks wisdom, you should ask God, who gives generously to all without finding fault, and it will be given to you. But when you ask, you must believe and not doubt, because the one who doubts is like a wave of the sea, blown and tossed by the wind." (James 1:2-6 NIV)

"Blessed is the one who perseveres under trial because, having stood the test, that person will receive the crown of life that the Lord has promised to those who love him." (James 1:12 NIV)

Having "pure joy" in times of trouble can be a very hard concept to grasp. What we need to realize is joy is not a feeling that comes and goes. Happiness is a feeling based on the circumstances that are happening around us. Joy is a fruit that comes from God as we know He

Day 3: Regaining Our Strength

is working in the trials and as we trust Him to strengthen us through our perseverance.

✝ What does James say comes through perseverance during trials?

_____

_____

✝ Has someone been a good example of having joy in the face of hardship? What stood out to you about how they expressed the pure joy of the Lord despite their circumstances?

_____

_____

_____

✝ How do you personally receive strength from the Lord?

_____

_____

_____

_____

The Prophet Isaiah writes in Isaiah 40:31 that those who wait for the Lord "…shall mount up with wings like eagles; …run and not be weary; …walk and not faint." In this passage, the eagle symbolizes youthful vigor and stamina. But how do we regain our strength and stamina after seasons of hardship that leave us tired and weary?

The Apostle Paul explains a pattern that occurs in the process of gaining strength whenever we face hardships in Romans 5:3-5, "Not only that, but we rejoice in our sufferings, knowing that suffering produces endurance, and endurance produces character, and character produces hope, and hope does not put us to shame, because God's love has been poured into our hearts through the Holy Spirit who has been given to us."

Rejoice in suffering -> Endurance -> Character -> Hope

It's hard to imagine rejoicing in our sufferings, but this is where our perspective shift produces strength. As we draw closer to the Lord and keep our eyes fixed on Him rather than the worldly solutions to our problems, we live with eyes of faith rather than what we see (2 Corinthians 5:7). The Lord increases our endurance and builds our character as we become more like Christ. And through this journey, we experience the hope found in the Lord. This hope gives us the strength to run the race set before us (Hebrews 12:1-3).

✝ Read Colossians 2:6-7 in your Bible and write it in the space below.

_____

_____

_____

_____

_____

When we are rooted in Christ and live in Him, He builds and strengthens us. In that strength, our lives overflow with our testimony of thankfulness for all He has done to lift our heavy burdens. And as we express the joy and thankfulness we experience in God's sustaining strength, others see His glory shining bright in our lives.

APPLICATION

✝ Think about the struggles you are facing right now. Circle where you are in the pattern below that the Apostle Paul gave us in Romans 5:3-5.

Rejoicing in Suffering -> Increasing Endurance -> Building Character -> Living in Hope

✝ In the space below, reflect on where you are in this pattern.

___

Heavenly Father, there are times when the light of Your love appears to dim within me as I focus more on the solutions the world offers for my burdens. Thank You for renewing my strength and increasing my endurance as I refocus and look to You. Help me be a bright shining light that displays Your glory and love through joy and thanksgiving in life's hardships. In Jesus's name, amen.

DAY 4

Remaining Clear-Headed and Watchful as We Move Forward in Hope

📖 A NOTE FROM LIFE

I recently watched a video of two gazelles locked in a fight, horn to horn. While a herd of gazelles watched the battle, danger lurked unnoticed. Far off in the distance, a lion eyed the gazelles, and unbeknownst to them, the lion closed the distance and pounced, killing one. The distraction of the fight placed the whole gazelle herd, including those fighting, in danger.

When we allow the struggle of carrying our burdens to distract us, we put ourselves at risk of being overwhelmed by the enemy and unable to fulfill the work the Lord has called us to do. Today, you will study scripture that will remind you of the importance of remaining watchful for the enemy's schemes as you humble yourself and rest in the Lord's lighter load so that you can live in the hope of His restoration and strength.

📖 SCRIPTURE STUDY

In 1 Peter 5:6-10, Peter cautions us not to become distracted by our cares and concerns but to remain clear-headed and watchful because the enemy lurks around like a lion, ready to pounce when we aren't paying attention.

Day 4: Remaining Clear-Headed and Watchful as We Move Forward in Hope

✝ Read 1 Peter 5:6-10 in your Bible. In the space below, write 1 Peter 5:6-7. Underline any words or phrases that stand out.

_____

_____

_____

_____

Peter encourages us to humble ourselves under God's mighty hand. The Greek word for "humble," *tapenienoo*, means to "lower, depress one's soul, bring down one's pride, to submit oneself in a lowly spirit to the power and will of God." This is the same word Luke uses in Luke 14:11 when he writes, "...those who humble themselves will be exalted."

Throughout this study, you've learned the importance of releasing your burdens before the Lord so that He can carry the heavy load for you. Theologian David Guzik states in his commentary on 1 Peter 5, "we cannot do God's work when we are weighed down by our burdens and worries. Cast them upon Him, and then take up the Lord's burden – which is [a] light burden, and a yoke that fits us perfectly."[x]

When we humble ourselves and release the concerns that distract us, we are freed from the weight we aren't meant to carry and lifted up or exalted to do the work the Lord has called us to do.

The Amplified version of 1 Peter 5:8-9 states, "Be sober [well balanced and self-disciplined], be alert and cautious at all times. The enemy of yours, the devil, prowls around like a roaring lion [fiercely hungry], seeking someone to devour. But resist him, be firm in your faith [against his attack – rooted, established, immovable], knowing that the same experiences of suffering are being experienced by your brothers and sisters throughout the world. [You do not suffer alone.]."

✝ How does Peter describe the actions of the devil?

_____

_____

_____

_____

✝ How does Peter tell us we should respond to the devil's actions?

_____

_____

_____

As we cast our burdens upon the Lord, we learn the importance of going to Him in times of trouble. Relying on the strength of the Lord's yoke enables us to withstand the enemy's attacks.

✝ In the space below, write out 1 Peter 5:10.

_____

_____

_____

_____

Peter acknowledges that we will go through seasons of suffering. However, we can take comfort in the fact that he also tells us they won't last forever. Our Heavenly Father is full of grace and desires to carry our heavy load and bring us into a new season of hope on the other side. God will restore, confirm, strengthen, and establish us in this new season of hope.

Day 4: Remaining Clear-Headed and Watchful as We Move Forward in Hope

✝ In the chart below, I have provided the Greek word and its definition of how God will bring us into a new season. Highlight any parts of the definitions that resonate with you.

God will	Greek word	Definition
restore	katartizō	"to strengthen, perfect, complete, make one what he ought to be"[xi]
confirm	stērizō	"to strengthen, make firm, to render constant, confirm, one's mind, establish"[xii]
strengthen	sthenoō	"to make strong, strengthen one's soul" note—this is the only time this word is used in the New Testament[xiii]
establish	themelioō	"to make stable, establish, settle the soul, lay the foundation"[xiv]

I love the Amplified version of 1 Peter 5:10, "After you have suffered for a little while, the God of all grace [who imparts His blessing and favor], who called you to His own eternal glory in Christ, will Himself complete, confirm, strengthen, and establish you [making you who you out to be]."

✝ It's easy to struggle with our faith when we go through hard seasons. But this passage teaches us that God will strengthen our souls to help us endure. Reflect on how God has strengthened your faith during times of challenge.

_____

_____

_____

_____

† Write a prayer thanking the Lord for taking your burdens upon Himself and using the hard seasons of your life to restore, confirm, strengthen, and establish you.

_____

_____

_____

_____

✋ APPLICATION

Friend, I know I've mentioned this many times throughout this study, but I want to reiterate it because I don't want you to miss this important point.

You weren't meant to carry the burdens that weigh you down.

Our Heavenly Father has a purpose and plan for your life. But you can't live according to His will for your life when you are distracted by what you aren't meant to carry. My hope and prayer are that you see the new season of hope the Lord is moving you into as you allow Him to restore and perfect you, making you who He created you to be.

† How have you experienced the Lord settling your soul as you stand firm on His solid foundation and move forward in the hope of how He has called you to serve Him?

_____

_____

_____

_____

Heavenly Father, thank You for having a purpose and plan for my life. And thank You, that as I humble myself and release my burdens to You, You restore me to who You made me to be, You confirm Your plans for my life, and You strengthen and settle my soul. Thank You for the hope I have moving forward as I carry Your light load. In Jesus's name, amen.

DAY 5

Review and Reflect

Heavenly Father, thank You for seeing my weakness as I tried to carry a load that was too heavy for me to carry. Thank You for calling me to You and willingly taking my heavy burden upon You and teaching me how to find hope in Your light load. Help me display Your joy and the strength that comes through You as I follow Your leading. In Jesus's name, amen.

Congratulations, my friend, you've completed the final week of *Come to Me*. Now, let's review our final week together.

† On day one, when you struggled to know how to pray, you learned to find rest in the hope and peace of the Holy Spirit and Jesus as they intercede to your Heavenly Father on your behalf.

† On day two, you learned to fix your eyes on the eternal glory that lies ahead, rather than focusing on your temporary sufferings so that your life can shine the light of Christ in your weakness as you experience true joy found in Him.

† On day three, you learned how to regain the light of your spiritual strength that has been dimmed by the influence of the world as you trust God to sustain you in His strength.

† On day four, you studied scripture that reminded you of the importance of remaining watchful for the enemy's schemes as you humble yourself and rest in the Lord's lighter load so that you can live in the hope of His restoration and strength.

Day 5: Review and Reflect

APPLICATION

Take a few minutes to review how the Lord spoke to you each day. Write out the passage that spoke to your heart this week.

† Journal a prayer to the Lord based on the passage above.

_____

_____

_____

_____

_____

_____

† Review your daily application questions and journal how the Lord has provided you with the inner strength you need as you learn to release your burdens to Him. Or if there is a burden you still struggle to release to the Lord, journal your thoughts on that struggle.

_____

_____

_____

_____

_____

Study Review and Reflection

Congratulations, my friend! I'm so proud of you for saying yes to Jesus's invitation to find rest for your soul. I pray you are experiencing the renewed joy and strength of learning to release your burdens as you take up the Lord's light yoke. Let's take a few minutes to review what you've learned these past four weeks.

✝ Review day five of each week and journal your biggest takeaway or aha moment with God.

_____

_____

_____

_____

_____

✝ What passage spoke most clearly to your heart through this study?

_____

_____

_____

_____

Here are a few scriptures for further study on finding God's rest.

- ✝ Psalm 139:17-18
- ✝ Matthew 6:6-13
- ✝ John 16:33
- ✝ Ephesians 6:10-18
- ✝ Hebrews 4:14-16

Heavenly Father,

Thank You for my sweet friend and her willingness to accept Your invitation to find rest for her soul. Thank You for calling us to You and loving us so much that You sent Your Son, Jesus, to rescue us from a life of sin. And thank You for Your Word, which teaches us how to come to You and release the burdens that weigh us down. As we continue to trust You with our grief, worry, and pain, help us stand taller as the weight is lifted off our shoulders. Strengthen us as we keep our eyes focused on Your glory and live each day in the hope and joy found in You. In Jesus's name, amen.

A Final Word

Friend, I have a confession to make. I'm struggling as I write this conclusion. Last night, something happened that turned my world sideways, and today, life feels heavy. It's frustrating because I had begun to feel true peace, rest, and joy that I haven't felt in a long time. Today, I feel like I've detached myself from Jesus's yoke and fallen back into my old habits of struggling under the weight of carrying my burdens again.

In my quiet time this morning, I shared that frustration with the Lord. The Lord graciously reminded me that He hasn't gone anywhere and is ready to help me carry this load of frustration, hurt, and worry.

Why am I telling you this?

Because I want to let you know I'm far from perfect. Remember, I wrote this study as part of my own exploration of Jesus's invitation to rest. You and I have come a long way as we've studied God's Word. But there will be moments when we revert to our natural tendencies and attempt to carry the weight of hard seasons on our shoulders. Our shoulders will slump under the heaviness of life, and we will seek the rest and joy we've enjoyed while trusting the Lord with our burdens.

And friend, when we find ourselves back in the same old place of not releasing our burdens to the Lord, He is kind, gracious, and ready to take our burdens upon Himself again. We have hope because we now have the tools to help us recognize if we are taking our burdens upon ourselves before we become too overwhelmed and exhausted. Each time we release our worries and concerns, it will get easier as we become better at relying on His strength.

So, in these last few moments together, I want to leave you with some encouragement Jesus shared with the disciples during their final hours with Him. In John 16:20, Jesus told the disciples, "Truly, truly, I say to you, you will weep and lament, but the world will rejoice. You will be sorrowful, but your sorrow will turn to joy." Jesus knew He was going to the cross in His ultimate display of taking our burdens and sins upon Himself. The disciples didn't fully understand all that would take place. But Jesus encouraged them to take heart. They would weep and mourn because of Jesus's death, but in God's perfect timing, they would see Him again, and their hearts would rejoice, and no one could take the complete joy they found in Jesus Christ (John 16:22-24).

As you and I accept Jesus's invitation to come to Him through salvation, we begin to trust Him as we lay our burdens before Him, abide in Him daily through studying His Word, take up His light yoke, and experience His peace and rest. In this, we are encouraged by the true joy that comes through Jesus.

I would love for you to share with me how this study impacted you. You can reach out via Instagram (@maryinhiscalm) or on Facebook (The Calm of His Presence).

Acknowledgments

Jeff: You are my biggest encourager and supporter. Thank you for believing in me even when I didn't believe in myself. I thank God every day for answering the prayers of a young girl and giving me a husband who is a strong man of God and leads our family faithfully. I love you!

Garrett and Caroline: Being your mom is the greatest gift and calling the Lord has ever given me. I'm so thankful God gave me a front-row seat to watch you grow into amazing young adults. Thank you for the many ways you have encouraged me. I love you both!

Mindy, Jenny, and the Flourish Writers Community: I am forever grateful for the wisdom and guidance you have given me in my writing journey. Thank you for walking alongside me, keeping me focused, and encouraging me to keep making progress. I couldn't have done this without you!

Marissa: I am so grateful the Lord brought us together through our sweet writer friend Brooke. Your friendship has been such a blessing to me on this journey. Thank you for the edits on other projects that have helped me become a better writer.

Ruth R., Denise S., Courtney J., Alicia H., Julie C., and Marie M.: Thank you for always being a source of encouragement and prayers. Your love and support mean the world to me!

Women of The Well: Thank you for your prayers and for always asking how things were going with the study. I can't wait to share this with you at a beach retreat!

Leader Guide

Roughly sixteen years ago, I felt the Lord calling me into women's ministry. In all honesty, I had no idea what that looked like. I had never been involved in a women's ministry at a local church. But, despite my uncertainty and feelings of complete inadequacy, I said yes to God and decided to take my first tentative step down the brand-new path God had called me to. I invited a few friends into my home and facilitated my very first Bible study. What better study to start with than Lysa TerKeurst's book, *Becoming More than a Good Bible Study Girl*?

Now, almost two decades later, I've facilitated countless Bible studies in my home and as a women's ministry leader at my local church. The beautiful thing is that the Lord has taught me valuable lessons as I've faithfully followed Him every step of the way.

Whether you are facilitating your very first group or are a seasoned veteran, I'm so thankful that you have chosen *Come to Me: An Invitation from Jesus to Find Rest for Your Soul*. I'm praying for you as you lead and minister to the ladies in your group.

GROUP PREPARATION

1. Pray – Prayer is the essential foundation as you gather your group and lead each week. Ask the Lord to bring women who need to experience the true rest that is found in Him. Set aside time during each meeting for brief prayer requests so that you and the rest of the group can pray over specific needs. It may be helpful to provide notecards for the group to keep track of prayer requests.

2. Create a welcoming environment - During your first meeting, consider providing simple snacks and coffee to foster a time of fellowship, allowing people to get to know each other before the study begins. Another important aspect of starting well is sharing expectations that each member will work through the study during the week, while giving grace that someone may have a hard week and not be able to complete the study. Encourage them that they are still welcome to attend because they can still learn something from the discussion.

3. Prayer - Acknowledge that a time of prayer will be included during each meeting. Some people may feel uncomfortable praying in a group setting. Encourage the women that prayer is one of the ways to help women grow deeper in their walk with the Lord. Explain that they are not required to pray but are encouraged to try sharing a short prayer in the small group at least once.

3. Facilitating discussion – As the group leader, you can choose how you want the discussion to flow. You can use all the questions in this guide or none of them. But consistency is key. Be prepared and guide the conversation equally among group members, while respecting the allotted time for the group meeting.

WELCOME WEEK

1. Begin the session with a time of fellowship to allow the women the opportunity to get to know one another.

2. Invite the women to introduce themselves and share briefly why they have joined the study.

3. Provide an overview of the study, along with the expectations for participation, and that what is shared in the discussions will remain confidential within the group.

4. Turn to page 8 and review the different translations of Matthew 11:28-30. Invite the ladies to share which translation speaks to their heart the most and why.

Leader Guide

5. Review the list on page 9 and ask the ladies to share their vision of true rest for their soul.

6. Close with prayer requests and prayer.

WEEK 1 – COME TO ME

1. Welcome the ladies and provide a brief overview of the week.

2. Invite the ladies to share their biggest takeaway from their week of personal study.

3. Follow up with questions drawn from the week's study.

    † What does it mean to know that God loved YOU so much that He gave His only Son to die on the cross for your sins? (p. 4)

    † What commonality do you see in Luke 23:44-46, Psalm 31:5, and Acts 7:59-60? (p. 13)

    † Review the list of burdens that weigh heavily on your heart and share if there are any obligations you can commit to handing over to someone else this week. (p. 15)

    † What was the promise of rest in Hebrews 4:1-11? (p. 19)

    † What do you imagine heaven will be like in contrast to the struggles you face today? (p. 22)

    † Have there been times when you have felt like an outcast? If you were the Samaritan woman at the well with Jesus, how would you feel if He acknowledged you and asked for a drink? (p. 25)

4. Wrap up discussion and ask for prayer requests.

5. Pray and dismiss.

WEEK 2 – TAKE MY YOKE UPON YOU

1. Welcome the ladies and provide a brief overview of the week.

2. Invite the ladies to share their biggest takeaway from their week of personal study.

3. Follow up with questions drawn from the week's study.

   † Read 1 John 5:1-5. First John 5:2 says, when we love God, we will obey His commandments. In verse three, it says that His commandments aren't burdensome. Do you believe that God's commandments aren't burdensome? (p. 35)

   † How can we gain victory over the burdens that weigh us down? (p. 37)

   † Do you place more significance on your kids' success or who they are becoming in Christ? (p. 38)

   † How does the realization that the Lord knows you so intimately make you feel? (p. 42)

   † How does knowing that you are never far from the Lord's presence comfort you? (p. 43)

   † How does knowing God created and is familiar with every aspect of who you are strengthen you? (p. 44)

   † Read Matthew 6:25-34 in your Bible. In this portion of Jesus's Sermon on the Mount, what did He tell us to do in times of worry? (p. 47)

   † How do you seek God in your time of need? (p. 48)

   † Look back over David's expressions of despair. Which of these resonates with you? What other feelings have you experienced in seasons of despair? (p. 53)

Leader Guide

† According to Psalm 91, what does God promise His children? (p. 55)

† How has the Lord shepherded and drawn near to you as you've begun to release your burdens to Him? (p. 58)

4. Wrap up the discussion and ask for prayer requests.

5. Pray and dismiss.

WEEK 3 – LEARN FROM ME

1. Welcome the ladies and provide a brief overview of the week.

2. Invite the ladies to share their biggest takeaway from their week of personal study.

3. Follow up with questions drawn from the week's study.

   † Read John 13:12-17 again. What lesson did Jesus want them to learn? (p. 63)

   † How do you need to find comfort and rest in the Lord in your current season? (p. 70)

   † What emotions or thoughts go through your mind as you think of being so close to your Heavenly Father during the storms of life that you can hear His heartbeat? (p. 72)

   † In Matthew 10:26-31, why did Jesus tell the Apostles not to fear? (p. 74)

   † Reflect on a time of need in your life. Did you sense God's presence then? If not, do you now see how God provided for and shepherded you through that need? How does the awareness of God's presence in your life help you know Him better? (p. 75)

   † List ways that you've personally experienced God's work in your life through God's characteristics of sovereignty, our Rock and Protector, and source of courage. (p. 78)

- † List the evidence of God's nearness in Psalm 34:14-22. (p. 80)

- † Who are you as you walk through seasons of adversity? Are you the servant who sees the obstacles through the eyes of fear? Or are you David and Elijah, and see with eyes of faith as you praise and trust the Lord in the storm? Or maybe some of both? (pp. 81-82)

4. Wrap up the discussion and ask for prayer requests.

5. Pray and dismiss.

WEEK 4 – FIND REST FOR YOUR SOUL

1. Welcome the ladies and provide a brief overview of the week.

2. Invite the ladies to share their biggest takeaway from their week of personal study.

3. Follow up with questions drawn from the week's study.

   - † Read Romans 8:34-39 in your Bible. Who sits at the right hand of God, interceding for us? (p. 90)

   - † Read Romans 8:26-27. What does the Spirit do for us? (p. 91)

   - † Reflect on a particularly good season of your life or a particularly bad season. How did that season help you experience God more deeply? For instance, what characteristic of God did you experience in that season? (p. 92)

   - † Why does Paul say we should not lose heart? (p. 97)

   - † What do our "light and momentary troubles" achieve for us? (p. 97)

   - † What are we to fix our eyes on and why? (p. 98)

   - † How have you seen and experienced the Lord's renewal as you've released your burdens to Him? (p. 99)

- ✝ As you think about the greatness of God, how does it make you feel to know He created you and knows you by name? (p. 101)

- ✝ What does James say comes through perseverance during trials? (p. 103)

- ✝ How do you personally receive strength from the Lord? (p. 103)

- ✝ It's easy to struggle with our faith when we go through hard seasons. But 1 Peter 5:10 teaches us that God will strengthen our souls to help us endure. Reflect on how God has strengthened your faith during times of challenge. (p. 109)

- ✝ How have you experienced the Lord settling your soul as you stand firm on His solid foundation and move forward in the hope of how He has called you to serve Him? (p. 110)

4. If time allows, close with the group's biggest takeaway or aha moment with God as they released their burdens to God during this study.

5. Wrap up the discussion and ask for prayer requests.

6. Pray and dismiss.

[i] https://www.preceptaustin.org/matthew_1128-30_commentary

[ii] https://www.preceptaustin.org/matthew_1128-30_commentary

[iii] https://www.preceptaustin.org/matthew_1128-30_commentary

[iv] https://www.preceptaustin.org/matthew_1128-30_commentary

[v] (Walvoord and Zuck 1985)

[vi] Guzik, D. "Study Guide for 1 Peter 5 by David Guzik." Blue Letter Bible. Last Modified 6/2022. https://www.blueletterbible.org/comm/guzik_david/study-guide/1-peter/1-peter-5.cfm

[vii] Guzik, D. "Study Guide for Isaiah 40 by David Guzik." Blue Letter Bible. Last Modified 6/2022. https://www.blueletterbible.org/comm/guzik_david/study-guide/isaiah/isaiah-40.cfm

[viii] "H2617 - ese - Strong's Hebrew Lexicon (esv)." Blue Letter Bible. Accessed 26 Nov, 2024. https://www.blueletterbible.org/lexicon/h2617/esv/wlc/0-1/

[ix] Witmer, John A. "Romans." Essay. In *The Bible Knowledge Commentary An Exposition of the Scriptures*, New Testament., 473. Wheaton, Illinois: SP Publications, 1983.

[x] Guzik, D. "Study Guide for 1 Peter 5 by David Guzik." Blue Letter Bible. Last Modified 6/2022. https://www.blueletterbible.org/comm/guzik_david/study-guide/1-peter/1-peter-5.cfm

[xi] "G2675 - katartizō - Strong's Greek Lexicon (esv)." Blue Letter Bible. Accessed 26 Nov, 2024. https://www.blueletterbible.org/lexicon/g2675/esv/mgnt/0-1/

[xii] "G4741 - stērizō - Strong's Greek Lexicon (esv)." Blue Letter Bible. Accessed 26 Nov, 2024. https://www.blueletterbible.org/lexicon/g4741/esv/mgnt/0-1/

[xiii] "G4599 - sthenoō - Strong's Greek Lexicon (esv)." Blue Letter Bible. Accessed 26 Nov, 2024. https://www.blueletterbible.org/lexicon/g4599/esv/mgnt/0-1/

[xiv] "G2311 - themelioō - Strong's Greek Lexicon (esv)." Blue Letter Bible. Accessed 26 Nov, 2024. https://www.blueletterbible.org/lexicon/g2311/esv/mgnt/0-1/

Author Bio

Mary Boswell loves the caffeine jolt of early morning coffee and brisk walks with Greta, her Weimaraner. But, she is also fully content pulling weeds in her garden, hiking in the mountains, or sitting in a chair with her feet in the ocean. Mary and her husband are learning to navigate the first stages of empty-nest life and dreaming of what's to come. Through life's twists and turns, Mary has learned the importance of keeping her heart focused on the Lord and seeking His calming presence through Bible Study and prayer.

You can connect with Mary on Instagram: @Maryinhiscalm, or her website: The Calm of His Presence, www.thecalmofhispresence.com, where she is passionate about helping women live in the middle of God's Word.

www.ingramcontent.com/pod-product-compliance
Lightning Source LLC
Chambersburg PA
CBHW071225090426
42736CB00014B/2975